Techno-Sapiens in a Networked Era

Techno-Sapiens in a Networked Era

Becoming Digital Neighbors

EDITED BY

Ryan K. Bolger

AND

Kutter Callaway

CASCADE *Books* • Eugene, Oregon

TECHNO-SAPIENS IN A NETWORKED ERA
Becoming Digital Neighbors

Cascade Books
An Imprint of Wipf and Stock Publishers
199 W. 8th Ave., Suite 3
Eugene, OR 97401

www.wipfandstock.com

PAPERBACK ISBN: 978-1-7252-8052-6
HARDCOVER ISBN: 978-1-7252-8053-3
EBOOK ISBN: 978-1-7252-8054-0

Cataloguing-in-Publication data:

Names: Bolger, Ryan K., editor. | Callaway, Kutter, editor.

Title: Techno-sapiens in a networked era : becoming digital neighbors / edited by Ryan K. Bolger and Kutter Callaway.

Description: Eugene, OR: Cascade Books, 2020 | Includes bibliographical references.

Identifiers: ISBN 978-1-7252-8052-6 (paperback) | ISBN 978-1-7252-8053-3 (hardcover) | ISBN 978-1-7252-8054-0 (ebook)

Subjects: LCSH: Technology—Religious aspects—Christianity. | Social media—Religious aspects—Christianity. | Theological anthropology.

Classification: BT741.3 .T40 2020 (print) | BT741.3 (ebook)

Manufactured in the U.S.A.   11/02/20

To all the neighbors, both digital and otherwise, who have helped us become more fully human.

Contents

Contributors

Ryan K. Bolger is Associate Professor of Church in Contemporary Culture at Fuller Theological Seminary.

Kutter Callaway is Associate Professor of Theology and Culture at Fuller Theological Seminary.

Heidi A. Campbell is Professor of Communication at Texas A&M University.

Pauline Cheong is Professor of Communication at Arizona State University.

Ilia Delio, OSF, is Connelly Chair in Christian Theology at Villanova University.

Angela Williams Gorrell is Assistant Professor of Practical Theology at Baylor's George W. Truett Theological Seminary.

Madison Kawakami Gilbertson is a recent doctoral graduate of Fuller's School of Psychology, focusing her research on virtue, character development, and interracial interactions.

Noreen Herzfeld is the Nicholas and Bernice Reuter Professor of Science and Religion at St. John's University and the College of St. Benedict and a research associate with ZRS Koper.

Sarah Schnitker is Associate Professor of Psychology and Neuroscience at Baylor University.

Acknowledgments

As an edited volume, this book represents the work of a multitude of people. We would like to thank each of the colleagues who contributed to this piece of scholarship, both for their intellectual rigor and their participation in the 2019 Techno-Sapiens conference at Fuller Seminary. In each and every case, the authors of these essays are stellar scholars in their own right who are leaders in their field. We would also like to thank the Henry Luce Foundation for supporting the conference, as well as the Center for Missiological Research, including Nelson Kiamu, who not only helped us with formatting the manuscript, but also delivered a stellar sermon to kick off our conference proceedings. Finally, we are thankful to Amos Yong, now Dean of the School of Mission and Theology and Chief Academic Officer at Fuller Theological Seminary, for his support and encouragement along the way. He was an advocate from day one, and the project would not have been realized without his support and encouragement.

Won't You Be My (Digital) Neighbor?

Ryan K. Bolger & Kutter Callaway

The increasingly rapid pace at which modern technology continues to develop and proliferate has fundamentally reshaped the whole of human life, perhaps nowhere more so than in the domain of religion. Indeed, the need for a robust and constructive response to the transformative effects of technology is now more urgent than ever. On the one hand, emerging technologies have the capacity to expose otherwise disconnected individuals and communities to a rich diversity of religious expressions across the globe, providing unparalleled access to the cultural and religious other and, by extension, serving as potential mechanisms for empathetic engagement and understanding. On the other hand, the psychological, commercial, and even algorithmic structures of these technologies not only create the conditions for, but also actively promote various forms of solipsism, partisan rancor, and radicalization almost exclusively along ideological lines. Neither the math nor the moneyed interests care about how we treat our neighbors in the digital world or whether our portrayals of them are remotely accurate, just so long as we keep "liking" that which reinforces our preconceived assumptions and "sharing" our fear-based outrage with like-minded friends.

In this kind of technologically mediated context—one in which "impressions" and "engagements" are the most valuable commodities—how might Christians be and become neighbors in ways that leverage the potential of modern technology while also countering its destructive tendencies? This introductory chapter will raise these questions by describing the contemporary era in which this theme has become important and, in doing so, will provide historical and missiological context. It will also seek to introduce the various chapters and, insofar as possible, integrate the argument that emerges.

The Media Is the Mission

Fifty years ago, innovations and convergences in technology created the elements of what would become a networked global society. Innovations included the *Arpanet* developed by the US in 1969, designed with the goal to develop a computer network with no center, one that would be immune to a Soviet attack. Other developments included digital switching of phone networks and the creation of the modem. In Sunnyvale, California, the birthplace of the semiconductor industry twenty years prior, Intel developed the microprocessor in 1971. Within five years, members of the Home Brew Computer Club in Sunnyvale, Steve Jobs and Steve Wozniak, built their first computer, the *Apple I*. For another home-built computer, the *Altair*, Bill Gates and Paul Allen wrote their first software program. In what would become known as *Silicon Valley,* the right ingredients existed for a "milieux of innovation."[1] Over the next twenty years, these developments made their ways into businesses and homes worldwide. What was birthed was a new type of society, economy, and culture.

The impact of Global Information Culture is now unparalleled, as the vast majority of the world has connections to each other and to the Internet primarily through mobile devices. Every arena of the human endeavor has experienced a revolution of sorts through the introduction of new technologies into its particular sphere. But these massive technological upheavals have done more than simply change the way human individuals and human societies relate to one another. Human life is now fundamentally augmented by technology, blurring the lines between the human and the machine. Some celebrate these advances. Others are haunted by visions of a post-human techno-future. Either way, it is becoming increasingly

---

1. The story of the beginning of the beginnings of the Information Technology Revolution is told by Manuel Castells, *The Rise of the Network Society*, 40–65. A "milieux of innovation" refers to the idea that technological change does not occur in a vacuum but arises in specific contexts where industry, users, and producers share their high-level knowledge and skills in defining and solving problems in a context where economic interests come into play and there is an openness to learning by doing. Castells, *The Rise of the Network Society*, 36–37.

clear that technological change is not simply about technological machinery. It's about what it means to be human.

Over sixty years ago, Donald McGavran, founder of the School of World Mission and Institute of Church Growth at Fuller Theological Seminary in Pasadena, California, advocated, against Western Christendom forms of ecclesial life, that indigenous church expressions be initiated for all peoples within their own groups, location, and culture. For three generations students have been trained in these particular skills as they serve as missionaries throughout the Earth. However, in the network society, humans live not as groups, but as networked individuals.[2] They no longer live their lives in a particular place, but abide in the space of flow.[3] And they are inhabitants not of a traditional culture, but rather live in the mediated space of real virtuality.[4] Needless to say, loving one's neighbor—the core driver of Christian mission in the world—may look quite different in the Network Society.[5] In this particular volume we explore the changed landscape of what it means to digitally love our (often digitized) neighbor.

From the earliest days of the Christian faith, the followers of Jesus were to imitate the way Jesus served and forgave others in his confrontation with the Powers. They were to love their neighbors. To love one's neighbor one would need to be fully engaged in cultural life. Jesus did not stand outside the practices of his day, e.g. table fellowship (convivial life centered in a common meal), but he fully participated in ordinary cultural practices, transforming them from within through love. Likewise, engaged Christians today do not choose the governing practices in which they participate, as if they could stand outside culture. Technological practices already exist as God's mediating structures (the Powers) and the church's task is to transform these practices, as insiders. Transformative engagement manifests differently in every type of practice, keeping in mind the church does not impose its way from a place of power, but comes to each practice as Jesus did—as a servant. Thus, while remaining faithful to the call to love and to forgive, the life of Christian communities (and how they care for their neighbors) may be expressed in novel ways in the space of flows (mediated digital space).

2. Rainie and Wellman, *Networked*, 6, 7.

3. Castells, *The Rise of the Network Society*, 376–428.

4. Castells, *The Rise of the Network Society*, 327–75.

5. Castells, *The Rise of the Network Society*, 60.

What is lacking is an understanding of how the radical changes effected in these numerous domains connect and relate to one another. What is required is collaboration between technological and theological minds in order to make connections across disciplines that will generate deeper understandings of our Networked epoch and how technological advances inform the mission of the church in 2020 and beyond. The time has come to host conversations between theology and technology—to begin to explore how Christian theology and missiology might be stretched to include interactions with Global Information Culture and its many manifestations: transhumanism, AI, Internet memes, Big Data, and virtue-based Apps, to name a few.

Being and Becoming Techno-Sapiens

Techno-Sapiens is devoted to engaging opportunities and challenges related to these many spheres. It gathers together leading scholars of technology, theology, and religion in order to explore the ways in which modern technology is neither solely a dehumanizing force in the world nor a mere instrument for evangelizing the world, but rather the very means by which incarnation happens—the media in and through which human bodies love the (digital) other.

Taken as a whole, the essays explore the following concerns as their starting points, each of which is oriented around the question of how technology encourages and/or inhibits the human capacity to love our neighbor:

1. Who is my (digital) neighbor? And for that matter, who am I? How have recent technological changes shaped humanity in general and what have been the implications of recent developments, specifically Transhumanism and Artificial Intelligence, for "techno-sapiens" more specifically?

2. How does social media in particular allow us to love our (digital) neighbor? What are the implications of social media platforms (and their tendency towards facilitating less-than-civil interaction between faiths), as well as of Big Data, for cultural and cross-cultural life more specifically, and what are the implications as such for Christian practice?

3. How does one become a (digital) neighbor? What is the impact of technological changes on the practice of character formation in

general and what are the implications of such especially for Christian communities as it pertains to Christian witness in the world?

Who is my (digital) neighbor?
And for that matter, who am I?

In addressing the first of these questions, Part I takes a closer look at who our digital neighbors are, and, perhaps more importantly, who we are digitally. In her chapter "Religion and Posthuman Life: Teilhard's Noosphere," Ilia Delio argues that technology has become embedded in human life itself. She wonders if transhumanism, in its focus on its own digital enhancement, fosters a truncated understanding of the role of humanity in the world. She acknowledges that Artificial Intelligence invites people to enhance their own lives, but it does not include personal transformation that leads to compassion and forgiveness. It is the spiritual practice of going beyond oneself, reaching out to God in and through material reality, that will give humans the ability to solve the problems of Earth, but this is not what transhumanism offers.

Descartes paved the way for a post-biological future, one that reduces the essence of humans to mind alone. Transhumanism takes up the same philosophical move. Delio, however, says no to the transhumanist vision that conceals a white, male, Eurocentric logic. She also refuses the Cartesian separation of mind from matter that is inherent in transhumanism. Finally, Delio says no to the transhuman hope that disembodied minds will be downloaded into machines as neuro-chips as soon as the year 2045.

Delio asserts that mind and matter are intertwined and mutually grow together. Against transhumanism, she advocates what Teilhard calls ultra-humanism. Consistent with Teilhard, Delio says yes to posthumanism and its vision of embodied humans working with machines to move evolution and themselves forward. Posthumanists, in contrast to transhumanists, celebrate the end of the autonomous subject and the birth of the deeply relational self. In this scenario, humans, in partnership with machines, jointly become something new as they connect to all creation through the obliteration of fixed differences. Human personhood is stretched into a complexified wholeness that crosses material boundaries. Race, gender, and being are constantly renegotiated through the splice, through deep interconnection with machine life. Humans merge with these machines as they extend themselves.

Somewhat in contrast, Noreen Herzfeld, in her chapter "A New Neighbor or a Divisive Force?," is skeptical of the human capacity to harness the forces of AI for good. In her view, humans have a somewhat naive view of technology influenced by Hollywood, with robots who help, think, and act like us. Robots offer humans a faithful friend who serves as a faithful companion. However, as Herzfeld asserts, neither robots nor AI itself are our neighbors. Robots do not feel any emotions (nor will they ever) and AI exists in constantly running algorithms controlling our lives and restricting our freedom. AI/robots are not neighbors but are often malevolent forces that make loving our actual neighbors much more difficult.

It is empathic (even agapic) love that enables humans to differ from robots. Humans exist in a web of loving relationships—in a series of I-thou connections. Humans embody the image of God when they are in relationship with others, according to Herzfeld. Robots cannot treat the other as a Thou. Beyond eliminating many of our jobs and life decisions, AI will not tell us when we need to step away from technology to become human and to bind up the broken-hearted. Neither robots nor AI can meet the requirements of being in relationship.

To be a neighbor, Herzfeld states, drawing on Barth, one must be able to do four things: look the other in the eye, speak and hear the other, aid the other, and to do it all gladly. The Good Samaritan in the Gospels meets the Barthian requirements for a neighbor, hence, Christians practice a faith that is neighborly at its very core. The Christian faith is inherently incarnational: God took on a human body in Jesus. Through living and dying, God relates to humanity's plight. The suffering of the embodied Christ expressed love, through presence, to all of creation, humans included. Transhumanism, manifesting itself through AI, fails to love the neighbor, human or otherwise.

How does social media in particular allow us to love our (digital) neighbor?

Part II narrows in focus, exploring how social media allows us (or not) to love our digital neighbor, specifically our religious neighbors. Heidi Campbell, in her chapter, "When Religious Internet Memes about Religion are Mean," writes that memes create a context that is fraught with stereotypes and truncated stories that serve as microaggressions. Memes encourage a hostile approach to the other, even towards uncivil action. Memes exist in the sphere of lived religion. They attempt to communicate everyday lived reality through images. Those who are the objects of these depictions experience them as hurtful and promoting hate. Memes spread rapidly online thereby quickly defaming and dehumanizing the religious other.

Campbell explores how memes depicting Muslims pass on bias against them based on stereotypes. She demonstrates that memes aimed at Muslims assert that they are angry Arabs, that they oppress their own women, and that Islam is anti-American. The memes also decry how liberal American leaders are naive about Islam's true intent. These Islamophobic stereotypes are not new, but they are given new expression and new life online. These religious memes are typically produced by outsiders, do not contain nuance, and they seek to reduce the religious other through a single image and phrase. Memes create reductionistic caricatures of another religion, in this case, Islam.

Christian leaders may want to consider how to help their congregants through asking questions such as "what message does the meme portray, and how might we respond?" Campbell advocates that these memes might serve as a point of dialogue in order to increase digital neighborliness and demonstrate compassion for the religious other both online and offline. She imagines that dialogue regarding memes might demonstrate care and love for the other.

Pauline Cheong, in her chapter "Data, Discernment, and Duty: Illuminating Engagement in the Internet of Things," discusses the innovations that live with us in our smart homes, churches, neighborhoods, and even embedded in our bodies. She explores how the datafication of everything impacts how we live. To be sure, church and mission leaders rely on large-scale data derived from sociological and anthropological studies. Numbers help church leaders simplify the tasks before them.

However, Cheong writes that, for some Christian leaders, the ends justifies the means, e.g., if data helps lead people to spiritual growth, then why not use it? Church members might feel liberated as Big Data gives rise to more custom church programming. However, the analyzed data responding to their choices might be considered manipulative rather than nurturing. Moreover, what are the privacy concerns when the gathering of data does not involve direct interaction with the subjects of the study, but instead is mined through massive aggregations of data generated online?

New data creates economic challenges for churches as well. The accumulation of data may be burdensome as the responsibility of reporting and acting on data increases the workload of church staff. Finally, what are the economics of these Big Data practices? For instance, do members pay to get access to the best spiritual growth opportunities?

Datafication privileges some while disadvantaging others. Cheong points out that data gathering and analysis is never a neutral activity but comes already politicized, mirroring existing power relations and exclusions. She clarifies that even raw data is a misnomer, as it is often massaged even before it is first presented in order to align with existing power relations. As church and mission institutions begin to rely on Big Data for their strategic planning, power relations within those organizations undergo a shift: those with access to new data gain power while those without access lose it.

The question of who my neighbor is gets more complex as I relate to others through the Internet of things. An assemblage of software governs the reporting of each person's spiritual life. New data unites and divides people based on the nature of what is collected. Every time an app is updated it redefines who is in and who is out depending on the value each data point is given. Given the expanded ability of research firms to mine personal data, the question arises: can Big Data help me better love my neighbor?

How does one become a (digital) neighbor?

The third question (how does one become a digital neighbor?) is the focus of part III. How is it that we might be formed, in positive ways, to love the other? What are the opportunities for character formation that leads to a Christian public witness in this new media landscape? And, ultimately, how do we become the very neighbors we would seek to be? Is there a way for character or spiritual formation to occur that would transform us into better digital neighbors?

Sarah Schnitker, Kutter Callaway, and Madison Kawakami Gilbertson demonstrate how a virtue focus to technology might facilitate positive character outcomes such as patience. Most frequently, we hear how technologies challenge and compromise our very character, but Schnitker, Callaway, and Kawakami Gilbertson in "Positive Youth Development and Technology: Developing Character in Youth in the Present Technological

Landscape," write that positive moral outcomes may be developed through the use of technology. Through interventions with technology, they research whether youth can experience character formation through the use of the app "Character Me."

The authors rightly note that technological interventions may seem counterintuitive. To help youth love their neighbors we would first need to get them off their cell phones! In contrast to a privation-based approach, the researchers did not ask the youth to leave their own personal world but created modes of transformation within their everyday life. The researchers' focus on virtue development through habit and embodied practice put recent theological innovations regarding virtue, character, and practice at the service of psychological and spiritual formation through technology.

Schnitker, Callaway, and Kawakami Gilbertson created an app-based solution that yielded positive virtue-based shifts in actual youth behavior. They tested this app on a diverse set of high school students in the Los Angeles area. The authors tentatively assert that this use of technology offers evidence of the collaborative work of the Spirit in the world. How so? "Character Me" increases the patience of the user, and patience with the other is one definitive aspect of loving one's neighbor. Because of this research, we might extrapolate broader still: can we now say that well-designed technology can improve how we function as neighbors, i.e., how we love in the world? The implications of technology in service of Christian love, as demonstrated by Schnitker, Callaway, and Kawakami Gilbertson are profound and point to the need for further research in this area.

Angela Gorrell also helps us in our thinking about how to become a better neighbor. In her chapter "The Quest to Become More Human: Christian Witness & the Transhumanist Movement", she questions how transhumanism can provide a viable future for humanity when it denies that death will continue to exist. She questions the values of transhumanism, especially in its different notions regarding what the good life is, not to mention its aspirations for well-being and its differing notions of life's purpose.

Gorrell explores how it is that Christians might be public witnesses in contemporary culture, one that has been so impacted by transhumanism. She unpacks witness to include what *beholding* and *telling* look like in six spheres of contemporary culture: meaningful ends, the body, suffering, inequality, technology design, and "interested conversation." She rightly notes that the ends of transhumanism and Christian faithfulness differ. One focuses completely on the self and the other on loving the other.

Gorrell writes that transhumanism puts forth a highly reductionistic vision: humans are conscious minds and nothing more. With the high value Christians place on incarnation, Gorrell argues that the differing notions of bodies puts transhumanism and Christianity at opposite ends of the spectrum. Moreover, the transhumanist goal to end all human suffering significantly differs from the Christian understanding that suffering may be a redemptive pattern of human life (while not advocating unnecessary suffering in any form).

Gorrell writes that the technological advances advocated by transhumanists may breed great social and economic inequality between those who can afford enhancements and those who cannot. However, Gorrell is more activist than Luddite: Christians must use their prophetic voice and speak against Big Tech's contrasting views of the good life, advocating instead for technology that supports the Christian vision of human flourishing. Gorrell does not deny that the Spirit is working in the technological world; she would just like to see "interested conversations" that address many of the issues just named in order to discern the way forward. In this way, Christians can properly witness, i.e., tell and behold, the flourishing life God created for all to experience.

Love as Interface

A common theme that emerges in these essays is that, by asking the question who my neighbor is, we discover philosophical, theological, and missiological resources for answering the inverse question of who (or rather what) my neighbor is not. My neighbor is not mind/consciousness alone attached to an incidental body, nor is my neighbor part of a disembodied supermind. My neighbor is not the autonomous liberal sovereign subject of the Enlightenment, nor is my neighbor an algorithm or robot.

So, who is my neighbor? My neighbor is one whose very identity is distributed across machines, creatures, species, and matter. My neighbor's subjectivity is co-emerging with mind and matter, flesh and silicon. My neighbor is an embodied relational self and mind, and my neighbor's biology is a core part of who they are. Finally, my neighbor is a cyborg.

How do I become a neighbor? To become a neighbor is to see the other as just like me. To see the other as a subject. To see my neighbor as a cyborg. To see the neighbor as a distributed subject across life, machines, and nature. To become a neighbor I do not see them as object nor Cartesian subject, but as distributed subject and deeply connected to me. To be a neighbor I see my neighbor as embodied, one who can suffer, one who I must not exclude or economically marginalize.

My neighbor is deeply interconnected with all people, machines, being and nonbeing. My neighbor lives through technology as it extends their own engagement with the world. From within, my neighbor is being continually drawn towards others to greater levels of love, complexity, and consciousness. My neighbor is constantly renegotiating all difference such as race, gender, nature, and machine.

I love my neighbor through technology because we are both connected to the splice which makes us one. I love my neighbor because where I stop and they begin is quite blurry: if I am to love myself I need to love my digital neighbor and vice-versa. My neighbor and I are not just connected at the level of mind or technology but in our underlying physical reality as well. To love my neighbor is to recognize that my own analog and digital evolution is bound up with theirs.

I am not a neighbor when I treat my religious other as an object, not a subject. I am a neighbor when I refuse to reduce their complexity as a human in any way. I love my neighbor when I see them as fully embodied and fully distributed across all divides. To love my neighbor is a refusal to manipulate them, to use them for making money, to diminish them, or to hurt them in any way. My neighbor is not the sum of the data that has been collected on them, and I recognize their right to own their own data. I become a better neighbor through initiating dialogue regarding ways Christians might prevent any sort of dehumanization of the other or to reduce the other into a singular definition.

To become a neighbor I must treat my other like the Good Samaritan did: to look the other in the eye, to speak and hear the other, to aid the other, and to do it all gladly. To become a neighbor I use technology to make me a better person, and thus a better lover of others. I become a neighbor when I yield to the Love that exists at the core of me and at the core of them, that draws me forward to desire union with all others, both living and nonliving.

My neighbor is a Techno-Sapien, just like me. I love my neighbor by accepting the fluid subjectivity of other Techno-Sapiens and when I choose to see both of us as deeply intertwined. I become a better neighbor by using technology to be more expansive in my love for my neighbor, and by depending on technology to make me a better human.

For both Luddites and technophiles, these are the background conditions that constitute life in contemporary society. Technology has the potential to arrest the development of our humanity. But technology also has the potential to enhance every aspect of our lives. It can and often is the site where incarnation happens. And it is this incarnational site that each of the essays in this volume explores—the technological interface that brings our bodies and our neighbors' bodies together in love.

Bibliography

Castells, Manuel. *The Rise of the Network Society, the Information Age: Economy, Society and Culture Vol. I.* Oxford: Blackwell, 1996.

Rainie, Lee, and Barry Wellman. *Networked: The New Operating System.* Cambridge, MA: MIT Press, 2012.

Part I

Who is my (digital) neighbor? And for that matter, who am I?

CHAPTER 1

Religion and Posthuman Life

Teilhard's Noosphere

ILIA DELIO

Artificial intelligence (AI) is one of the most significant new sciences of the twentieth century. Born from insights on cybernetic systems, machine thinking, and information, AI now dominates the cultural terrain personally and globally. We are enamored by its powers but frightened by its possibilities. How do we adequately assess the role of AI in human life? Can AI enhance human relationships and build communities or are we inventing machines that will eventually cause human extinction? By contextualizing the rise of AI within the larger historical context of evolution we can begin to define a more integrated role for AI in the emergence of human personhood. This paper will examine the emergence of AI in the midst of the violent twentieth century and the significance of this development for a new philosophy of personhood. I will explore two trajectories of AI that support different philosophical positions: transhumanism and the emphasis on human betterment and posthumanism and the quest for deep relationality. Using the work of John Johnston and Katherine Hayles, I will examine the significance of posthumanism as new levels of consciousness and complexity. I will suggest that a new type of person is emerging with posthumanism, one that corresponds to the insights of Teilhard de Chardin and his ideas on ultrahuman life in the Noosphere. Teilhard's evolutionary paradigm gives direction to posthuman/ultrahuman life in which religion plays a significant role. I will explore his insights on religion and evolution and suggest new ways to develop it for planetary life.

The Emergence of AI Life

In his book *The Allure of Machinic Life,* John Johnston argues that in the early era of cybernetics and information theory following the Second World War, two distinctively new types of machine appeared. The first, the computer, was initially associated with war and death—breaking secret codes and calculating artillery trajectories and the forces required to trigger atomic bombs. But the second type, a new kind of liminal machine, was associated with life, inasmuch as it exhibited many of the behaviors that characterize living entities—homeostasis, self-directed action, adaptability, and reproduction. Neither fully alive nor at all inanimate, these liminal machines (thinking machines) exhibited what he calls "machinic life," mirroring in purposeful action the behavior associated with organic life while also suggesting an altogether different form of "life," an "artificial" alternative, or parallel, not fully answerable to the ontological priority and sovereign prerogatives of the organic, biological realm. These forms of machinic life are characterized not by any exact imitation of natural life but by complexity of behavior.

Johnston questions if the new biological-electronic hybridization or machinic life is an extension of "nature" life. He states, "our human capacity as toolmakers (*homo faber*) has also made us the vehicle and means of realization for new forms of machinic life."[1] He continues by saying that artificial life is actually producing a new kind of entity or being that is at once technical object and simulated collective subject. He writes:

> Constituted of elements or agents that operate collectively as an emergent, self-organizing system, this new entity is not simply a prime instance of the theory of emergence, as its strictly scientific context suggests. It is also a form of artificial life that raises the possibility that terms like subject and object, physis and techne, the natural and the artificial, are now obsolete. What counts instead is the mechanism of emergence itself, whatever the provenance of its constitutive agents.[2]

---

1. Johnston, *The Allure of Machinic Life*, 12.
2. Johnston, *The Allure of Machinic Life*, 13.

Johnston identifies "becoming machinic" as the process of cyborgization, a process of increasing levels of hybridity between human and nonhuman life forms. The term *cyborg* emerged in the 1960s with space travel and the need to maintain human physiological function in nonhuman environments of outer space. The cyborg (or cybernetic organism) is a mixture of biology and machine whereby the machine enables biological function. The emergence of the cyborg signals the fact that nature's boundaries are not fixed but fluid. Nature is a co-creation among humans and nonhumans, machines and our other partners. The two narratives that Johnston highlights reflect the two trajectories of AI: Shallow AI or radical Transhumanism and Deep AI or Posthumanism. Each posits a different philosophical perspective of the human person. While they are not exactly conflicting positions, since aspects of transhumanism are also found in posthumanism, they differ philosophically.

Transhumanism

The word *transhumanism* was initially coined by Julian Huxley to describe novelty in evolution; however, philosopher Nick Bostrom seized upon transhumanism as the technological salvation of modernity's failure to achieve social change: "In the postwar era, many optimistic futurists who had become suspicious of collectively orchestrated social change found a new home for their hopes in scientific and technological progress."[3] He began the World Transhumanist Association in 1998, with David Pearce, as a cultural and philosophical center of human betterment through technology. A corollary group known as Extropy (a philosophy devoted to the transcendence of human limits) was founded by Max More, who immigrated to California from Britain and changed his name from Max O'Connor to Max More. More founded the Extropy Institute to catalyze the transhuman ideal of betterment: "I was going to get better at everything, become smarter, fitter, and healthier . . . a constant reminder to keep moving forward."[4] Following the closure of the Extropy Institute in 2006, *Humanity+* emerged as an outgrowth of the World Transhumanist Association and has since become the principal representative of the transhumanism movement.

---

3. Bostrom, "A History of Transhumanist Thought," 7.
4. Regis, "Meet the Extropians," 10.

We aim to deeply influence a new generation of thinkers who dare to envision humanity's next steps. Our programs combine unique insights into the developments of emerging and speculative technologies that focus on the well-being of our species and the changes that we are and will be facing. Our programs are designed to produce outcomes that can be helpful to individuals and institutions.[5]

Since its inception, the World Transhumanist Association, along with the pioneering work of Extropy Institute, has contributed to advancing the public knowledge of how science and technology can and will affect our human future. Hence "transhumanism" now refers to those technologies that can improve mental and physical aspects of the human condition such as suffering, disease, aging, and death, "the belief that humans must wrest their biological destiny from evolution's blind process of random variation . . . favoring the use of science and technology to overcome biological limitations."[6] Ray Kurzweil, for example, anticipates an increasingly virtual life in which the bodily presence of human beings will become irrelevant. Kurzweil claims that machine-dependent humans will eventually create the virtual reality of eternal life, possibly by "neurochips" or simply by becoming totally machine dependent. As we move beyond mortality through computational technology, our identity will be based on our evolving mind file. We will be software not hardware. By replacing living bodies with virtual bodies capable of transferral and duplication, we will become disembodied superminds.[7] Robert Geraci states, "Our new selves will be infinitely replicable, allowing them to escape the finality of death."[8]

This futuristic "post-biological" computer-based immortality is one also envisioned by Hans Moravec, who claims that the advent of intelligent machines (*machina sapiens*) will provide humanity with "personal immortality by mind transplant." Moravec suggests that the mind will be able to be downloaded into a machine through the "eventual replacement of brain

---

5. Transhumanist Technology, "About Humanity+," https://humanityplus.org/about/.

6. Bostrom, "History of Transhumanist Thought," 13–14; Archimedes Carag Articulo, "Towards an Ethics of Technology: Re-Exploring Teilhard de Chardin's Theory of Technology and Evolution," http://www.scribd.com/doc/16038038/Paper2-Technology.

7. Noble, *Religion of Technology*, 154. Ray Kurzweil defines the singularity as the point at which machines become sufficiently intelligent to start teaching themselves. When that happens, he indicates, the world will irrevocably shift from the biological to the mechanical. See Kurzweil, *The Age of Spiritual Machines*, 3–5.

8. Geraci, "Spiritual Robots," 235.

cells by electronic circuits and identical input-output functions."[9] Michael Benedikt believes that cyberspace is an extension of religious desires to escape earthly existence. The "image of the Heavenly City," he writes, "is . . . a religious vision of cyberspace."[10] The pursuit of cybernetic heaven means that we will be able to overcome the limitations of the body—including suffering and death—and attain artificial eschatological paradise. Just as human beings must give up their bodies to attain the heavenly city, so too AI transhumanists view relinquishing the human body for artificial mediums as a positive step in the evolution of *techno sapiens.*

Daniel Crevier argues that AI is consistent with the Christian belief in resurrection and immortality. Since some kind of support is required for the information and organization that constitutes our minds, Crevier indicates, a material, mechanical replacement for the mortal body will suffice. Christ was resurrected in a new body, he states, why not a machine?[11] Antje Jackelén notes that the development toward *techno sapiens* might be regarded as a step toward the kingdom of God. What else can we say when the lame walk, the blind see, the deaf hear, and the dead are at least virtually alive? The requirements of the gospel and the aims of technical development seem to be in perfect harmony.[12] Geraci states: "Only by eliminating the physical and embracing the virtual can we return to the undifferentiated wholeness of the good."[13]

Many transhumanists look to a postbiological future where super informational beings will flourish and biological limits such as disease, aging, and death will be overcome. Bart Kosko, a professor of electrical engineering at the University of Southern California, writes: "Biology is not destiny. It was never more than tendency. It was just nature's first quick and dirty way to compute with meat. Chips are destiny."[14] Similarly Robert Jastrow claimed, "human evolution is nearly a finished chapter in the history of life," although the evolution of intelligence will not end because a new species will arise, "a new kind of intelligent life more likely to be made of silicon."[15] While AI

9. Moravec, *Mind Children,* 110–11.

10. Benedikt, "Introduction," 16.

11. Crevier, *AI,* 278–80.

12 Jackelén, "The Image of God," 294.

13 Geraci, "Apocalyptic AI," 165.

14. Hook, "The Techno-Sapiens are Coming."

15. Cited in Theodore Roszak, "Evolution and the Transcendence of Mind," *Perspectives* 1.2 (1996). http://www.mentalhelp.net/poc/view_doc.php?type=doc&id=274.

transhumanists aim toward a new virtual body, they also anticipate a new virtual creation where the earthly garden will wither away and be replaced by a much greater world, a paradise never to be lost.[16]

Transhumanism is the legacy of the enlightenment's liberal subject whose Kantian motto *"sapere aude,"* dare to know, hangs like a banner over the dream of postbiological life.[17] The Cartesian subject is ripe for post-biological life. This narrow-minded, binary way of thinking is "shallow" because it fails to recognize the integral relationship between mind and matter, which evolve together as a complex whole. Transhumanism induces an "artificial" into intelligence by aiming to separate mind from body and eventually uploading mind into an artificial medium. Such an attempt at artificially separating mind and matter not only enhances fragmentation and disorder (which undergirds war and destruction) but this trajectory contradicts the evolutionary trend of convergence, whereby mind and matter complexify together.

The Rise of the Posthuman

While Transhumanism seeks betterment through technology, posthumanism seeks deeper relationality. Posthumanism or "deep AI" regards the person as a complex entity of embodied mind embedded in a matrix of cultural information. Katherine Hayles is the author of *How We Became Posthuman*, a highly sophisticated treatment of technology, embodiment, and personhood. She writes:

> Historically the idea of the liberal humanist subject, which was accompanied by notions of free will, autonomy, rationality, and consciousness as the seedbed of identity was deeply bound up with causal explanations in science. It was a science that was equipped to deal with a world in which there were weak or negligible interactions between different bodies and particles. These notions translated into the idea of an autonomous self, possessed of rationality and free will.[18]

In posthuman and new materialist thinking, matter is regarded as always already entangled with discourse in the enactment of phenomena.

---

16 Moravec, *Robot*, 143.

17. Bostrom, "History of Transhumanist Thought," 4.

18. Kroker, *Body Drift*, 11; Hayles, "Unfinished Work," 159–66 at 160.

The term "new materialism" was coined by Manuel DeLanda and Rosi Braidotti in the second half of the 1990s and refers to idea that mind is always already material and matter is necessarily something of the mind. Hence it builds on the inseparability of mind and matter. The complex interaction among multiple forces spawns and reconfigures in the new materialist and posthuman thinking. This reconfiguration occurs via conceptualizations of assemblages where the intra-activity and entangling agencies in and through material-discursive apparatuses point to comprehensive open-ended processes that undergird human identity and action. That is, the posthuman does not presume separateness of anything or any preexistent entities. Rather matter is agentive, "not a fixed property of things" but "generated and generative" so that nature and culture are entwined, agential, differentiating, and entangled. The posthuman signals a new type of relational person emerging in and through information embeddedness whose boundaries undergo continuous construction and reconstruction. A dynamic partnership between humans and intelligent machines is replacing the liberal humanist subject's manifest destiny to dominate and control nature. Hayles writes:

> The posthuman is likely to be seen as antihuman because it envisions the conscious mind as a small subsystem running its program of self-construction and self-assurance while remaining ignorant of the actual dynamics of complex systems. But the posthuman does not really mean the end of humanity. It signals instead the end of a certain conception of the human, a conception that may have applied at best to that fraction of humanity who had the wealth, power and leisure to conceptualize themselves as autonomous beings exercising their will through individual agency and choice.[19]

In the posthuman the distributed cognition of the emergent human subject correlates with the distributed cognitive system as a whole in which "thinking" is done by both human and nonhuman actors. Hence the posthuman ability to conceptualize oneself as autonomous being, exercising one's will through individual agency and choice, gives way to distributed personhood where conscious agency is never fully in control. In this respect, Hayles sees the liberal subject of the Enlightenment (supported by transhumanists) as coming to an end. In the posthuman, she states, "There are no essential differences, or absolute demarcations, between bodily existence and computer simulation, cybernetic mechanism and biological

19. Hayles, *How I Became Posthuman*, 286.

organism, robot technology and human goals."[20] She concludes with a death knell: "Humans can either go gently into that good night, joining the dinosaurs as a species that once ruled the earth but is now obsolete, or hang on for a while longer by becoming machines themselves. In either case . . . the age of the human is drawing to a close."[21]

Hayles and other new materialist philosophers indicate that the modern liberal subject is coming to an end. Information, cybernetics, and the rerouting of nature into new machinic life is giving rise to a new type of person. Unlike the binary liberal subject of transhumanism, posthumanism is cyborgian, materially extended life. Posthumanism redefines personhood in terms of cognitive assemblages. Continuous interaction with electronic devices does not ignore the human person as agent; however, agency is now reconfigured as distributed, interactive agential realism. Karen Barad uses the term "agential intra-action," meaning that what is pre-existing is relations from which relata (that which relates) emerge. Hayles ventures into a discussion on how information technologies fundamentally alter the relation of signified to signifier. She maintains that within informatics "a signifier on one level becomes a signified on the next-higher level."[22] She characterizes the bodily world as a world in which one can contrast presence and absence, and the virtual world of information technologies as a world in which one contrasts pattern and randomness.

Hayles masterfully argues for the significance of embodiment (in contrast to the transhumanist body as machine) for the formation of thought and knowledge. She writes: "Information, like humanity, cannot exist apart from the embodiment that brings it into being as a material entity in the world; and embodiment is always instantiated, local, and specific."[23] The body that "exists in space and time . . . defines the parameters within which the cogitating mind can arrive at 'certainties.'"[24] She reminds the reader that the body writes discourse as much as discourse writes the body. Briefly stated, embodied experience generates the deep and pervasive networks of metaphors and analogies by which we elaborate our understanding of the world. Hayles goes on to add that "when people begin using their bodies in significantly different ways, either because of technological innovations

20. Hayles, *How We Became Posthuman,* 2–3.

21 Hayles, *How We Became Posthuman,* 2–3

22. Hayles, *How I Became Posthuman,* 31.

23. Hayles, *How I Became Posthuman,* 48.

24. Hayles, *How I Became Posthuman,* 203.

or other cultural shifts, experiences of embodiment bubble up into language, affecting the metaphoric networks at play within culture."[25] In this respect, *electronic literature* can be understood as part of an ongoing attempt to direct posthumanism toward embodiment. Electronic language provides a type of embodiment, a distributed embodiment (my term) that rattles the liberal autonomous subject, drawing away from the idea of the disembodied person. She refuses received interpretations of the liberal human subject in favor of drawing radical lessons to be learned from the regime of computation. She explains that the posthuman is an emergent "reflexivity" in that human-machine complexity forms personhood and the person becomes part of the system it generates.

Hayles sees that the traditional relationship of human subjectivity *to* technology is undergoing a historic, perhaps cosmological, revision. She rejects the perspective of technological determinism (which evokes a humanist perspective) and celebrates technology as a new singularity. Ray Kurzweil also predicts a singularity by 2045, a point where human intelligence and machines will be welded in a seamless flow of mind, a transition point where machines will become smarter than people. For Kurzweil, the singularity is an opportunity for humankind to improve. "We're going to get more neocortex, we're going to be funnier, we're going to be better at music. We're going to be sexier," Kurzweil said during an interview. "We're really going to exemplify all the things that we value in humans to a greater degree."[26] Here is a fundamental difference, however, between the transhumanist and the posthuman: transhumanism emphasizes betterment anticipating a "super-intelligent life."

Posthumanism emphasizes deep relationality and entangled life. Hayles suggests that a new humanism is developing directly at the borderline of simulation and materiality. In her perspective, the scientific language of complexity theory—dissipative structures, fluidities, porous boundaries, and bifurcations—is projected beyond the boundaries of scientific debate to become the constitutive principles of a form of humanism enabled by the regime of computation. The grammar of the body is shifting from exclusive concern with questions of sexual normativity and gendered identity to a creative interrogation of what happens to questions of consciousness, sexuality, power, and culture in a computational culture,

---

25. Hayles, *How I Became Posthuman*, 206–7.

26. See https://futurism.com/kurzweil-claims-that-the-singularity-will-happen-by-2045.

in which the code moves from the visible to the invisible, from a history of tools and prosthetics external to the body to a language of simulation fully internal to identity formation.

Living from the Splice

Hayles's cultural achievement lies in a critical perspective on technology in which the human species limits itself to that of a "co-evolving" partner in the relationship and against the technical will to disembodiment and immateriality. Her writings point to the body's deep participation in the question of technology. Since the person as embodied mind is now extended electronically, personal identity finds a new locus. When the human is seen as part of a distributed system, the full expression of human capability is seen to *depend on the splice* rather than being imperiled by it. In this respect, identity is ongoing, constructive, intra-agential, and self-organizing. Drawing on Barad's agential realism, knowing is a matter of intra-acting. The term "intra-acting" refers to acting reciprocally, a term consonant with cybernetic systems. Information forms an intra-acting process of personal formation and world formation. Sharing information becomes an ontological performance of the world in its ongoing articulation and differential becoming. We are part of the world in its ongoing changes, reconfigurations, dynamics, production of meaning and entities (its ongoing intra-activity), and the world takes shape through our actions. Knowing and being, Barad claims, are mutually related: "We know because we are of the world. We are part of the world in its differential becoming."[27]

The posthuman therefore is no longer the liberal subject of modernity living from a will to power but the person who now *lives from the splice*, that is, the inter-material space between biology and machine/device, the intra-acting person whose subjectivity is embodied, embedded connectivity living from a new locus of identity, the "in-between" space of relationship itself. The logic of posthuman personhood is a logic of complexified relationships that opens a creative space of engagement. One lives not in a binary mode (*me* and *you*) but in the creative space of interrelatedness (me *and* you) so that relationships ontologize relata. One finds one's being not within oneself but beyond oneself (the beyond is within and the within is beyond), in the relationships that form oneself; the "I" flows from constitutive relationships of shared information. Being itself is a decentering and

27. Barad, *Meeting the Universe Halfway*, 76.

reforming flow that exists in creative tension with present existence and openness to novel form.

The dynamics of complexified relationships are nonlinear, unstable fluxes of ongoing engagement so that subjects are always emerging intra-personally and co-constitutively. What is posited here is the appearance of a becoming that is symbiotic, a hybridity of entities, a *tertium quid* that gives way to complexified being. The French philosopher Emmanuel Levinas employs triadic logic in his book *Otherwise Than Being* where he writes:

> It (triadic logic) is a relationship with a surplus always exterior to the totality, as though the objective totality did not fill out the true measure of being, as though another concept, the concept of infinity, were needed to express this transcendence with regard to the totality, non-encompassable within a totality and as primordial as totality.[28]

In triadic logic a limit is where Infinity overflows itself towards another and the limit must be included as part of the logic. Of course, taken at face value this seems absurd. But perhaps it is absurd because we think of logic as binary logic and therefore as a synchronized, totalized structure of relationality that cannot tolerate the ambiguity of the excluded middle. The logic of posthuman relationships follows a different trajectory from the modern liberal subject because the parameters of the cognitive system it inhabits expands and is multidimensional. Personhood is an open system of distributed subjectivity so that categories of gender, race, and religion are less defining and more negotiated ones. The human person is no longer the source from which emanates the mastery necessary to dominate and control the environment. Rather, "thinking" is done by both human and nonhuman actors. "Only if one thinks of the subject as an autonomous self, independent of the environment," Hayles claims, "is one likely to experience panic."[29]

While the lines of personhood are rewired in posthuman life, the question of human identity remains open. What constitutes "this" person in the matrix of hybridizing relationships? Even if relationships are intra-agential they are not completely random: why "this" relationship and not "that" one? What governs the ongoing co-constitutive relationality of emerging posthuman life? Is AI opening up pathways to a new collective consciousness so that the posthuman is part of a new type of collective

28. Levinas, *Otherwise Than Being*, 23.
29. Hayles, *How I Became Posthuman*, 290.

personhood oriented toward planetary life? Michael Burdett and Victoria Lorimar write: "Whereas certain transhumanists might lament the fact that we aren't solely in charge of our own destiny, critical posthumanists celebrate it and indeed argue we will never flourish if we don't first recognize that our relations with others are endemic to who we are. Hence, critical posthumanists argue for a deep and abiding relationality."[30]

Relationality, not betterment, is the operative word of posthuman life. Humans are part of a deep relational wholeness that is characteristic of nature itself. Complex dynamical thinking impels us to think of humans as integrated into wider systems of relationality. Burdett and Lorimar state: "What might make them distinctive is the extent to which other species and entities are implicated in this relationality and the way our formation and identities depend on them. It is not just other human beings that we 'become-with', to use the phrase of Haraway, but other creatures and artefacts, too."[31] By placing posthuman life in the context of evolution we can better appreciate how AI is complexifying consciousness and reshaping matter toward new levels of interrelated life.

Posthumanism, seen through the lens of critical feminists, interprets technology as the breakdown of boundaries, the fusion of disparate identities, and the forging of a new type of person electronically embedded in systems of information, including the systems of ecology, economics, and politics.[32] Posthumanism owes its very expression to a fundamental paradigmatic shift in the nature of scientific realism today. For Hayles, the scientific language of complexity theory—dissipative structures, fluidities, porous boundaries, and bifurcations—is projected beyond the boundaries of scientific debate to become the constitutive principles of a form of humanism enabled by hybridized electronic life.

Hayles's cultural achievement, Arthur Kroker suggests, "lies in suggesting a critical perspective on technology."[33] The human person becomes that of a "co-evolving" partner in the complexified electronic relationship. A dynamic partnership between humans and intelligent machines replaces the liberal humanist subject's manifest destiny to dominate and control nature. As Hayles states, navigating into the future does not have to be apocalyptic but takes place in the complex interactions within an environment

30. Burdett and Lordimer, "Creatures Bound for Glory," 241–53 at 249.

31. Burdett and Lordimer, "Creatures Bound for Glory," 249.

32. See Braidotti, *The Posthuman*, 13–25.

33. Kroker, *Body Drift*, 12.

that includes both human and nonhuman actors. The posthuman is best described as a complex dynamical system in which cybernetics governs ongoing negotiation of boundaries and choices. The human person is not simply the source of mastery over the environment in which technology is a tool for our use or an obstacle to our otherwise private solitary lives. Rather, the distributed cognition of the emergent human subject correlates with the distributed cognitive system as a whole electronic environment, in which "thinking" is done by both human and nonhuman actors. In the posthuman, human functionality expands because the parameters of the cognitive system it inhabits expands. Hayles states, "What is lethal is not the posthuman as such but the grafting of the posthuman onto a liberal humanist view of the self." For example, "You" choosing to download yourself into a computer, attaining the ultimate privilege of immortality.[34]

The posthuman is an expression of "deep AI," a new emergence of personhood through electronic embeddedness. AI extends the embodied mind into exoskeletal systems of information so that neither mind nor body disappear but are now complexified in systems which extend into larger maps of complexified wholeness electronically facilitated. The electronically embedded relational posthuman lives in the splices of informational fields so that boundaries of gender, race, and religion are transcended or rather constantly renegotiated through the creative space of shared being. Markers of intelligence are also shifting insofar as the brain is learning to adapt to multiple information fields. Super-intelligent machines will not replace us;[35] rather, we are transcending our present existence by merging with super-intelligent machines, giving rise to a new type of thinking person.

Teilhard's Noosphere

Posthumanism speaks to the search for a new ecology but the question in light of deep relationality is, where are we going? Transhumanism has a clear aim of human betterment. By improving ourselves with technology, we will become smarter, happier, healthier, and live longer, perhaps indefinitely. But the aims of posthumanism are not clear. If relationships are redefining personhood, toward what end?

34. Hayles, *How We Became Posthuman*, 286–87.

35. On the possibility of human extinction by super Intelligent machines see Charles T. Rubin, "Artificial Intelligence and Human Nature," *The New Atlantis*, https://www.thenewatlantis.com/publications/artificial-intelligence-and-human-nature.

The posthuman is being born in a chaotic world without meaning or orientation. Although the posthuman constructs meaning, what orients our direction or construction of meaning? Teilhard de Chardin was a scientist, involved in the discussions of how evolution proceeds with direction, and was influenced by the philosopher Henri Bergson's theory of creative evolution. Bergson rejected Darwinian evolution in that it failed to adequately account for novelty and transcendence in nature. He posited an élan vital in nature that could account for creative evolution. Bergson's ideas impelled Teilhard to form his principle of Omega as a way of explaining intrinsic wholeness and direction. "Omega" is the last letter of the Greek alphabet and has meaning in both science and religion because it signifies the end of something, its ultimate limit. Omega makes wholeness in nature not only possible but intensely personal because it is the most intensely personal center that makes beings personal and centered.[36] It is both in evolution and independent of evolution, within and yet distinct, autonomous and independent, deeply influential on the nature's propensity toward complexity and consciousness.[37] It is operative from the beginning of evolution, acting on pre-living cosmic elements as a single impulse of energy.[38] Teilhard posited that the Omega principle is a principle of attraction in *everything* that exists; it is irreducible to isolated elements yet accounts for the "*more* in the cell than in the molecule, *more* in society than in the individual, and *more* in mathematical construction than in calculations or theorems."[39] As the principle of centration, it is independent of nature, not subject to entropy, and ahead of nature as its prime mover. Omega emerges from the organic totality of evolution insofar as evolution proceeds to greater wholeness marked by higher levels of unity and consciousness; Omega is the goal toward which evolution tends.[40]

By positing Omega as the goal of evolution, Teilhard was not positing a supernatural force but an internal power that is simultaneously deeply present and overflowing nature itself. The Omega principle helps make sense of the direction of evolution toward more consciousness. Teilhard saw the process of evolution as a dynamic unfolding of mind and matter and the openness of these to greater complexity and consciousness. He spoke

36. Teilhard, *Activation of Energy*, 112.
37. Teilhard, *Phenomenon of Man*, 257–60.
38. Teilhard, *Activation of Energy*, 121.
39. Teilhard, *Phenomenon of Man*, 268.
40. Teilhard, *Activation of Energy*, 114.

of dual aspect to materiality, a withinness and a withoutness, conscious-ness and attraction, transcendence and unity, and identified love as the core energy that both transcends and attracts. Because all of nature bears the marks of transcendence and attraction, he spoke of love as a cosmological force, present from the beginning of the universe: "Love is the most univer-sal, the most tremendous and the most mysterious of the cosmic forces . . . the *physical* structure of the universe is love."[41] Love is a unitive energy, "the building power that works against entropy," by which the elements search their way towards union.[42]

There is an unyielding openness to biological and cosmic life that is not adequately explained by materiality, the orientation itself being "spirit" or energy overflow, an innate propensity of matter toward spirit. Teilhard saw this energy overflow of matter as the religious dimension of evolution. He wrote: "There is only one real evolution, the evolution of convergence, because it alone is positive and creative."[43] The openness of matter to spirit and the propensity of nature to complexify on higher levels of unity impelled Teilhard to posit that religion and evolution go together. Nature has an in-trinsic orientation toward wholeness, a horizon of complexifying wholeness oriented to a future anticipation of ultimate wholeness. Teilhard wrote: "To my mind, the religious phenomenon, taken as a whole, is simply the reaction of the universe as such, of collective consciousness and human action in pro-cess of development."[44] "Religion and evolution should neither be confused nor divorced," Teilhard wrote. "They are destined to form one single con-tinuous organism, in which their respective lives prolong, are dependent on, and complete one another."[45] By saying religion and evolution go together, Teilhard indicated that there is a capacity in cosmic life for more personal and unifying life. The centrating power of this emerging unity is God.

Theogenesis

Teilhard's God is one of creative union. If God is love, then the perfection of divine love includes the fulfillment of creation. God could not fulfill God's nature without some other to love. God creates in order to share God's life

41. Teilhard, *Human Energy*, 32.

42. King, *Mysticism of Knowing*, 104–5.

43 Teilhard, *Christianity and Evolution*, 87.

44. Teilhard, "How I Believe," 118–19.

45. Teilhard, *How I Believe*, 60–61.

and thus God and world are not opposed but complementary: God and world belong together and complete one another. Teilhard said that creation is integral to God. He believed that without creation, something would be absolutely lacking to God, considered in the fullness not of his being but of his act of union. God and world are in a process of creative union. Creation is unfinished and exists in a dynamic process of unification and God is unfinished in relation to the world growing in love.

Teilhard developed a doctrine of theogenesis (literally, the birthing of God) based on the rise of consciousness in evolution. If God is love and love is relational, God can only be the fullness of love through the deepening of relationships in evolution. He wrote: "As a direct consequence of the unitive process by which God is revealed to us, he in some way 'transforms himself' as he incorporates us."[46] As we come to a higher consciousness of a point of unity, God rises up in us; God *becomes* God in us. This is the meaning of incarnation; God "enters into" matter by rising up in matter as the unitive power of love. God is in us and we are in God without collapsing or merging these two realities, since they form a single reality. It is not enough to simply believe in God, Teilhard said; rather we are to incarnate God and help God become God, if we are to realize the potential of created existence.[47] As God rises up through higher consciousness, the human evolves from an incomplete whole to a new level of completion and thus a new vision, a new knowing, and a new way of acting in the world. Peter Todd writes:

> Like Jung, Teilhard thinks God needs humankind to become both whole and complete. The implication is that God and humanity are in an entangled state and that the individuation of each is inextricably bound with the other. This entanglement of God and world is symbolized by the concept of Omega. Teilhard develops an understanding of personalization whereby God becomes God in union with another because only in union with another can one's true personality be found.[48]

Since God is love and love is personal, center-to-center attraction, God is most deeply actualized in personal love. God loves in and through our love for one another. Only in actualization can love be experienced on a personal level, in the attraction and relations between one's deepest center, as it

---

46. Teilhard, *Hymn of the Universe*, 53.

47. Teilhard, *Hymn of the Universe,* 53.

48. Todd, *Teilhard and Other Modern Thinkers*, 5.

is drawn to another. The universe may be understood as God's actualization in deepening and personalizing love. As the most conscious point of the universe, the human person realizes God's life through the deepest, most personal love. Love causes God to be.

Noosphere and the Role of Love

Teilhard lived at the dawn of the computer and was fascinated by the computer as a new level of interconnecting minds. This new level, he said, is a new stage of convergence in evolution, the formation of what he called "the noosphere," a new level of coreflective thought and action.[49] In his *Phenomenon of Man* Teilhard describes the noosphere:

> The idea is that the Earth [is] not only becoming covered by myriads of grains of thought, but becoming enclosed in a single thinking envelope so as to form a single vast grain of thought on the sidereal scale, the plurality of individual reflections grouping themselves together and reinforcing one another in the act of a single unanimous reflection.[50]

Just as Earth once covered itself with a film of interdependent living organisms which we call the biosphere, so humankind's achievements are forming a global network of collective mind.[51] The noosphere is a psychosocial process, a planetary neo-envelope *essentially linked with the biosphere* in which it has its root yet is distinguished from it. Teilhard envisioned the noosphere as a global network of collective mind.[52] He saw evolution proceeding to a greater unification of the whole in and through the human person who is the growing tip of the evolutionary process. In his introduction to Teilhard's

---

49. Teilhard, *Future of Man*, 204. In the 1920s Teilhard coined the word *noosphere* in collaboration with his friend Edouard Le Roy. The noosphere (sometimes noösphere) is the sphere of human thought. The word derives from the Greek νοῦς (nous "mind") and σφαῖρα (sphaira, "sphere"), in lexical analogy to "atmosphere" and "biosphere." It was introduced by Pierre Teilhard de Chardin in 1922 in his Cosmogenesis. Another possibility is the first use of the term by Édouard Le Roy (1870–1954), who together with Teilhard was listening to lectures of Vladimir Ivanovich Vernadsky at the Sorbonne; cf. Ursula King, "One Planet, One Spirit: Searching for an Ecologically Balanced Spirituality," *Ecotheology* 10.1 (April 2005), https://journals.equinoxpub.com/index.php/JSRNC/article/view/1516.

50. Teilhard, *Phenomenon of Man*, 251.

51. Murray, *The Thought of Teilhard de Chardin*, 20–21.

52. Murray, *The Thought of Teilhard de Chardin*, 20–21.

Phenomenon of Man, Julian Huxley wrote, "We should consider inter-thinking humanity as a new type of organism whose destiny it is to realize new possibilities for evolving life on this planet."[53] Both Huxley and Teilhard saw this new type of person as a hyperpersonalizing person on a new level of "cooperative interthinking."[54] Just as human persons develop a complex brain, Teilhard saw that the earth is developing a "planetary brain," a global complex brain, made possible by computer-mediated interconnected minds. He posited a new type of person to embody this new type of brain, an "ultra" human whereby thought is no longer on the level of the individual but on the level of the convergent and collective.

Teilhard saw the hybridization of human and machine intelligence as completing the material and cerebral sphere of collective thought, and in this respect he is a forerunner of posthumanism.[55] His hopeful vision was a richer and more complex domain of matter and mind through the development of technology, a way of constructing or joining all minds together in a collective or global mind for the forward movement of cosmic evolution. In his *Heart of Matter* he wrote: "How can we fail to see that the process of convergence from which we emerged, body and soul, is continuing to envelop us more closely than ever, to grip us, in the form of . . . a gigantic planetary contraction?"[56] The individual human person, he thought, will be surpassed by a collective convergence of consciousness giving rise to the ultrahuman, a new person who is part of the new planetary consciousness.

To appreciate Teilhard's position is to realize that he was not enamored of technology as an autonomous power but technology as the main impetus of Omega-centered evolution. The ultrahuman is an effort to impel humanity to enter into its own evolution, that is, the value of technology is for the sake of spirituality. He wrote:

---

53. Teilhard, *Phenomenon of Man,* 20.

54. Teilhard, *Phenomenon of Man,* 21.

55. See for example Eric Steinhart, "Teilhard de Chardin and Transhumanism," *Journal of Evolution and Technology* 20.1 (2008) 22, http://jetpress.org/v20/steinhart. htm. Steinhart begins his paper by saying: "Teilhard was one of the first to articulate transhumanist themes. Transhumanists advocate the ethical use of technology for human enhancement. Teilhard's writing likewise argues for the ethical application of technology in order to advance humanity beyond the limitations of natural biology." However, Teilhard's transhumanism is cosmic evolution on the level of mind. In this respect he is closer to the position of posthumanism.

56. Teilhard, *The Heart of Matter,* 36.

> However far science pushes its discovery of the essential fire and however capable it becomes someday of remodeling and perfecting the human element, it will always find itself in the end facing the same problem—how to give to each and every element its final value by grouping them in the unity of an organized whole.[57]

Teilhard saw the insufficiency of science alone to effect the transition to superconsciousness and collective unity. "It is not tête-à-tête or a corps-à-corps we need; it is a heart to heart."[58] Technology for Teilhard is in the service of love as the deepest vital energy of the universe. He asks:

> Why do we not recognize in the accelerating totalization against which we are struggling, sometimes so desperately, simply the normal continuation at a level above ourselves of that process which generates Thought on Earth? Why do we not see that it is continuing the process of cerebration?[59]

Teilhard saw evolution of the posthuman/ultrahuman in terms of Lamarckian rather than Darwinian evolution, "the possibility of continuing improvement, passed on from one generation to another, in the actual *organ* of this vision."[60] The rise of the posthuman or ultrahuman represents a new collective consciousness that transcends individual consciousness and evokes a new type of person whose body now extends to the whole electronically mediated plane.

Hyperpersonalization

Teilhard did not live to see the technological revolution of the Internet but he imagined a thinking earth formed by the linking of electronic minds. The ultrahuman, like the posthuman, represents a new collective consciousness that transcends individual consciousness and evokes a new type of person whose body now extends to the whole electronically connected planet. Hominization continues in and with new lines of shared information. What is "staring us in the face," Teilhard wrote, is the rise of a "collective reflection" which is now realized to some extent by the Internet. As we increasingly emerge through complexified consciousness

57. Teilhard, *Phenomenon of Man*, 250.
58. Teilhard, *Future of Man*, 75; Kenny, *A Path through Teilhard's Phenomenon*, 138.
59. Teilhard, *Heart of Matter*, 37.
60. Teilhard, *Heart of Matter*, 37.

into posthuman/ultrahuman life, the concept of personhood is changing in accord with the new consciousness. He anticipated that each ego will be "forced convulsively beyond itself into some mysterious *super ego*."[61] This "super ego" reflects the notion that the individual is coming to an end and a new "hyper-personal" is emerging in evolution.

Only when the noosphere is aligned with the whole, the cosmos/universe, can it facilitate the *deeply personal* through *convergence* by bringing together consciousness, person, and creativity. Teilhard wrote: "The future universal cannot be anything else but the *hyperpersonal*."[62] This hyperpersonal for Teilhard is a "folding in" of consciousness, as if the lines of consciousness are merging together into one great complexified brain of planetary thought and planetary thought is giving rise to a new planetary body. This too is what Hayles conceives of in the posthuman, the electronically embedded person whose body is machine-body, whose ego is collective or super-ego and whose passion or emotional life must also be collectivized. The posthuman is the planetized conscious life whose new collective powers have the potential to form a new planetary whole.

What Teilhard contributes to the evolution of AI is a context for a new collective consciousness. In his view, this is an evolutionary leap toward a new world Soul, a unifying spiritual thread of interconnecting minds. The further evolution of humanity toward greater unity, he wrote, "will never materialize unless we fully develop within ourselves the exceptionally strong unifying powers exerted by inter-human sympathy and religious forces."[63] For Teilhard the noosphere is the newest realm of evolution where God is rising up. Technology has ushered in a new level of complexified consciousness where God is being born from within.

Conclusion

The posthuman hyperconnectivity that drives modern culture is not a drive for superintelligence but deep relationships. In Teilhard's terms, it is a drive for more profound union in love and a deepening of being: "It is not well-being but a hunger for more-being which can alone preserve the thinking earth from the tedium of life."[64] Teilhard distinguished "more-being"

61. Teilhard, *Heart of Matter*, 38.

62. Teilhard, *Phenomenon of Man*, 260.

63. King, *Teilhard and Eastern Religions*, 193.

64. Teilhard, *Future of Man*, 317.

from "well-being" by saying that materialism can bring about well-being but spirituality and an increase in psychic energy or consciousness brings about more-being.[65] He imagined psychic energy in a continually more reflective state, giving rise to ultrahumanity.[66] The Future universal cannot be anything else but the *hyperpersonal*."[67]

Teilhard's theogenesic evolution means we are responsible for the future and we are responsible for God. Reality is a process marked by a drive for transcendence and God is at the heart of transcendence. "When God is removed from nature," Philip Hefner writes, "God disappears, and when God disappears we disappear to our own selves because we are not our own making."[68] Transhumanism is alluring and the possibilities of living healthier, wealthier, and smarter play into the weakness of our frail human condition. But without a cosmic sacred dimension to our lives and a way of harnessing spiritual energies toward a transcendent convergent center of love, we are abandoned to the forces of capitalism and consumerism. Teilhard's vision helps us realize that religion is the most crucial factor for AI in the twenty-first century; without it we will be left fearful and vulnerable.

Bibliography

Barad, Karen. *Meeting the Universe Halfway: Quantum Physics and the Entanglement of Matter and Meaning.* Durham, NC: Duke University Press, 2007.

Benedikt, Michael. "Introduction." In *Cyberspace: First Steps,* edited by Michael Benedikt, 1–26. Cambridge, MA: MIT, 1991.

Bostrom, Nick. "A History of Transhumanist Thought." *Journal of Evolution and Technology* 14.1 (April 2005) 1–25.

Braidotti, Rosi. *The Posthuman.* Malden, MA: Polity, 2013.

Burdett, Michael, and Victoria Lordimer. "Creatures Bound for Glory: Biotechnological Enhancement and Visions of Human Flourishing." *Studies in Christian Ethics* 32.3 (2019) 241–53.

Crevier, Daniel. *AI: The Tumultuous History of the Search for Artificial Intelligence.* New York: Basic, 1994.

Geraci, Robert M. "Apocalyptic AI: Religion and the Promise of Artificial Intelligence." *Journal of the American Academy of Religion* 76.1 (2008) 138–66. www.jstor.org/stable/40006028.

———. "Spiritual Robots: Religion and Our Scientific View of the Natural World," *Theology and Science* 4.3 (2006) 229–46.

65. Grau, *Morality and the Human Future*, 275.

66. Kenny, *A Path through Teilhard's Phenomenon*, 105.

67. Teilhard, *Phenomenon of Man*, 260.

68. Hefner, *Technology and Human Becoming*, 83.

Grau, Joseph A. *Morality and the Human Future in the Thought of Teilhard De Chardin: A Critical Study.* Plainsboro, NJ: Associated University Press, 1976.

Hayles, Katherine N. *How I Became Posthuman: Virtual Bodies in Cybernetics, Literature, and Informatics.* Chicago: University of Chicago Press, 1999.

———. *How We Became Posthuman: Virtual Bodies in Cybernetics, Literature, and Informatics.* Chicago: University of Chicago Press, 1999.

———. "Unfinished Work: From Cyborg to Cognisphere." *Theory, Culture and Society* 23.7–8 (2006) 159–66.

Hefner, Phillip. *Technology and Human Becoming.* Minneapolis: AugsburgFortress, 2005.

Hook, Christopher C. "The Techno-Sapiens are Coming." *Christianity Today,* January 1, 2004. www.christianitytoday.com/ct/2004/january/1.36.html.

Jackelén, Antje. "The Image of God as *Techno Sapiens.*" *Zygon* 37.2 (2002) 289–302.

Johnston, John. *The Allure of Machinic Life: Cybernetics, Artificial Life, and the New AI.* Cambridge, MA: MIT Press, 2008.

Kenny, W. Henry. *A Path through Teilhard's Phenomenon.* Dayton, OH: Pflaum, 1970.

King, Thomas M. *Teilhard's Mysticism of Knowing.* New York: Seabury, 1981.

King, Ursula. *Teilhard de Chardin and Eastern Religions: Spirituality and Mysticism in an Evolutionary World.* Mahwah, NJ: Paulist, 2011.

Kroker, Arthur. *Body Drift: Butler, Hayles, Haraway.* Minneapolis: University of Minnesota Press, 2012.

Kurzweil, Ray. *The Age of Spiritual Machines: When Computers Exceed Human Intelligence.* New York: Viking, 1999.

Levinas, Emmanuel. *Otherwise Than Being.* Translated by Alphonso Lingis. Boston: Kluwer Academic, 1991.

Moravec, Hans. *Mind Children: The Future of Robot and Human Intelligence.* Cambridge, MA: Harvard University Press, 1988.

———. *Robot: Mere Machine to Transcendent Mind.* New York: Oxford University, 1999.

Murray, Michael H. *The Thought of Teilhard de Chardin.* New York: Seabury, 1966.

Noble, David F. *Religion of Technology: The Divinity of Man and the Spirit of Invention.* New York: Penguin, 1999.

Regis, Ed. "Meet the Extropians." *Wired,* October 1, 1994. https://www.wired.com/1994/10/extropians/.

Teilhard de Chardin, Pierre. *Activation of Energy.* Translated by René Hague. New York: Harcourt Brace Jovanovich, 1970.

———. *Christianity and Evolution: Reflections on Science and Religion.* Translated by René Hague. New York: Harcourt, 1971.

———. *Future of Man.* New York: Harper Collins, 1964.

———. *The Heart of Matter.* Translated by René Hague. New York: Houghton, 1979.

———. "How I Believe." In *Christianity and Evolution: Reflections on Science and Religion,* 118–19. Translated by René Hague. New York: Harcourt, 1971.

———. *How I Believe?* Translated by René Hague. New York: Harper & Row, 1969.

———. *Human Energy.* New York: Harcourt Brace Jovanovich, 1971.

———. *Hymn of the Universe.* New York: Fontana-Collins, 1973.

———. *The Phenomenon of Man.* New York: Perennial Library, 1975.

Todd, Peter B. *Teilhard and Other Modern Thinkers on Evolution, Mind, and Matter.* Woodbridge, CT: American Teilhard Association, 2013.

Transhumanist Technology. "About Humanity+." https://humanityplus.org/about/.

CHAPTER 2

AI: A New Neighbor
or a Divisive Force?

NOREEN HERZFELD

A lawyer once asked Jesus of Nazareth, "What must I do to live?"
Jesus replied, "What is written in the law?" The other answered,
"You shall love the Lord your God with all your heart, with all
your soul, with all your strength, and with all your mind; and your
neighbor as yourself." Jesus replied, "Do this and you will live."
This summation of the law raised the further question from the
lawyer, namely, "Who is my neighbor?" Have the answers to these
questions changed in our information age?

The term *AI* conjures images of the quasi-human figures of science fiction and film. Our digital creations have become more and more like us
these last few years. We carry on conversations with Siri and Alexa. Sophia,
an astonishingly lifelike robot, smiles, answers questions, and has been
given citizenship in Saudi Arabia. Japanese corporations hold welcoming
ceremonies for robotic receptionists. Machine learning programs now
teach themselves and come up with problem-solving strategies quite unlike
those of human experts, as we saw with Google DeepMind's AlphaGo, now
the reigning Go champion of the world. Do we now have a whole new set of
neighbors in AI? AI seems to give us something we innately desire—a nonhuman Other with whom we can relate as we relate to our fellow humans.
Has the neighborhood just gotten bigger?

I would say no, for two reasons. First, AI is less like us than we are led
to believe, in some crucial ways. As Christians, we believe we are created

in the image of God. An examination of what that means correlates with the passage from Luke quoted above. This image is best found in the love we exhibit for one another. Can a computer love? Not yet, nor likely in the future. Second, while the examples of AI given here are flashy and news-friendly, they are not the AI that currently saturates our world. We most frequently encounter AI not in some quasi-human or robotic form, but in faceless algorithms that aggregate our data and manipulate our behavior behind the scenes. This AI not only fails to be a neighbor to us but has proven, so far, to be adept at alienating and isolating us from the human neighbors we already have.

This presents for Christians a new call, one that asks us to see in AI not what we want but what is already there, to make better choices of what we do with our time, our talents, and our data, and to work even harder at loving our fellow humans as ourselves.

Who Are We? Humans as the Image of God

What a being that is wholly Other might share with humanity is not a question new to the computer age. This question is central to the theological concept of the *imago Dei* or image of God in which, according to Genesis 1, human beings were created. Interpretations of the *imago Dei* have varied, yet most can be categorized in one of three ways: substantive interpretations view the image as an individually held property that is a part of our nature, most often associated with reason; functional interpretations find the image of God in agency, specifically our exercise of dominion over the earth; relational interpretations locate God's image within the relationships we establish and maintain.[1] Approaches to developing an artificial intelligence have followed similar lines, looking first for intelligence as the property of an isolated machine, but more recently moving toward intelligence as demonstrated in either action or relationship. This similarity is not a surprise. It is the human that stands in the center, looking out toward both God and computer; the questions of what we share with God and

---

1. Some have looked for the *imago Dei* in a quality of the human being, such as our physical form (Gunkel), the ability to stand upright (Koehler), our rationality or intellect (Aquinas), our personality (Procksch), or our capacity for self-transcendence (Niebuhr). Others have thought of God's image as dynamic, rooted in human actions such as our dominion over the animals (Caspari, von Rad). A third approach defines the image as emergent in the interrelationship of two beings (Barth, Brunner). See Westermann, *Genesis 1–11*, 147–48 for a summary.

what we might share with an artificial intelligence are both rooted in an examination of our own human nature.[2]

Function as Image

The early church fathers followed Aristotle in seeing intelligence as the property we alone shared with God. This has several drawbacks. First, unlike Aristotle, we now know that we are not the only rational animal (λογικὸν ζῷον). Our primate cousins, dolphins, octopuses, even many birds exhibit a wide variety of capabilities we consider intelligent. Second, what is intelligence? We have no simple definition, thus look for it primarily in action. Finally, Genesis 1 says nothing about intelligence but a lot about stewardship. Thus, biblical scholars turned to an exegesis of the text itself, in the context of extrabiblical sources of the time for a better understanding of what God's image might be. Johannes Hehn was first to suggest that the image of God be understood as a royal title or designation rather than an attribute of human nature.[3] Old Testament scholar Gerhard von Rad was one of several who extended Hehn's work into a dynamic, functional approach to the *imago Dei*, one that locates the image not in a quality we possess, but in our agency or activity. In his commentary on Genesis, von Rad argues for our creation "as the image of God" rather than the usual "in the image of God."[4] Von Rad writes: "Just as powerful earthly kings, to indicate their claim to dominion, erect an image of themselves in the provinces of their empire where they do not personally appear, so man is placed upon earth in God's image, as God's sovereign emblem. He is really only God's representative, summoned to maintain and enforce God's claim to dominion over the earth."[5] This approach has come to dominate the field of Biblical exegesis and fits well with theologian Philip Hefner's understanding of human beings as created co-creators whose purpose is to exercise agency in the natural world. We are God's hands, effecting the transformation of the material world—co-creators, with emphasis on creator.[6]

---

2. For a full examination of this, see Noreen Herzfeld, *In Our Image*.

3. Hehn, "Zum Terminus 'Bild Gottes,'" in *Festschrift Eduard Sachau zum siebzigsten Geburtstag*, 36–52.

4. von Rad, *Genesis*, 56.

5. von Rad, *Genesis*, 58.

6. Hefner, *The Human Factor*.

A similar shift from intelligence as a property to a functional definition occurred in the field of AI in the 1980s. The attempt to capture human thought through symbolic logic, while producing some early results in easily modeled fields such as calculus or chess, failed to produce a general model for intelligence. This led to a move toward creating narrower expert systems. Rather than trying to replicate the human process of reasoning, functional AI exploits the speed and storage capabilities of the computer while ignoring those parts of human thought that are not understood or easily modeled. An example of a successful functional program is the chess playing program, Deep Blue, which defeated then world champion Gary Kasparov in 1997.[7]

Most AI today is functional, exercising agency for us in many realms. But these programs raise a question that is difficult to answer. What functions are crucial to intelligence? A definition that includes as AI any program that accomplishes some task human beings normally do would encompass virtually all computer applications, indeed, all human tools, but it would be ludicrous to consider all tools or all computers intelligent. For a functional approach to result in a full humanlike intelligence it would be necessary not only to specify which functions make up intelligence, but also to make those functions suitably congruent with one another. Computer programs are notorious for their differing approaches and inability to be joined together. Although a functional definition fits most current programs in AI, it leaves us with the uneasy feeling that something is missing, for we humans are more than the sum of our actions.

Relationship as Image

What is missing is precisely what Jesus put his finger on in the story from Luke. It is loving one another, being in relationship, which we share with God and hope to share with AI. Our agency is effective and blessed, rather than demonic, only when it is in partnership, first with God and then with one another. Indeed, the entire force of Genesis 4—10, the stories of Cain and Abel, the Tower of Babel, and the Flood, demonstrates the futility

---

7. Deep Blue does not attempt to mimic the thought of a human chess player but capitalizes on the strengths of the computer by examining more than 200 million moves per second, giving it the ability to look fourteen moves ahead. Deep Blue does not use intuition, and to know anything of its opponent's style, it must be reprogrammed for each opponent.

of relying solely on our own devices. The most influential proponent of
a relational interpretation of the *imago Dei* is Karl Barth. According to
Barth, the image of God is identified with the fact that the human being is
a counterpart to God.[8] Like the functionalists, Barth roots his argument in
textual exegesis, focusing, however, on two very different portions of the
Genesis text: "Let us make man in our image" (1:26) and "male and female
he created them" (1:27). Barth interprets the plural in "Let us make man" as
referring not to a heavenly court but to the Triune nature of God, a nature
that contains both an "I" that can issue a call and a "Thou" capable of response.[9] For Barth, this I-Thou confrontation forms the ground of human
creation, rooting human nature in relationship. The image of God is in the
relationship itself, not our capacity for relationship. Thus the image of God
can only be expressed corporately. It exists first in our relationship to God
and secondarily in our relationships with each other. Barth finds further
evidence for this interpretation in the person of Jesus, in whom he sees human nature as it was intended to be.[10] What Barth sees as significant about
Jesus is his relationships with God and with other humans. Barth notes: "If
we see Him alone, we do not see Him at all. If we see him, we see with and
around Him in ever widening circles His disciples, the people, His enemies,
and the countless multitudes who never have heard His name. We see Him
as theirs, determined by them and for them, belonging to each and every
one of them."[11] For Barth, it matters not so much what any human does, but
that we exist in a web of loving relationship.

Contemporary Western society strongly supports a functional approach, in which both our tools and our very selves are defined by what we
do.[12] We have many successful programs that do some task. Such functionality is easy to measure and produces results that contribute to our quality

8. Barth, *Church Dogmatics* III/1, 184–85. Barth lists and denies the variety of substantive and functional interpretations in vogue at his time: "The fact that I am born and
die; that I act and drink and sleep; that I develop and maintain myself; that beyond this I
assert myself in the face of others, and even physically propagate my sperm; that I enjoy
and work and play and fashion and possess; that I acquire and have and exercise powers;
that I take part in all the work of the race; and that in it all I fulfill my aptitudes as an
understanding and thinking, willing and feeling being—all this is not my humanity."
Church Dogmatics III/2, 249.

9. Barth, *Church Dogmatics* III/2, 182.

10. Barth, *Church Dogmatics* III/2, 88–89.

11. Barth, *Church Dogmatics* III/2, 216.

12. How often the first question asked on meeting someone is "What do you do?"

of life. However, so far, no particular program has been hailed as possessing intelligence. And defining ourselves in terms of what we do also suffers when applied to particular persons, making it all too easy to denigrate disabled members of the human family. My father suffered from Parkinson's disease. His agency was entirely diminished by the end. Did he image God in his past but cease to do so as he approached death? Is the homeless woman on the street less in God's image because she does not contribute to the creation of material wealth or the artifacts of culture? Is the helpless infant only potentially in the image of God? Instinctively, we answer these questions with a resounding "No!"

Our fears of being replaced by machines are also rooted in this functional paradigm. If dominion of the earth, as measured by the completion of tasks, were the center of our being, we would be right to fear the future. Machines will soon do much of our work for us. According to a 2019 Brookings Institution report, at least 36 million Americans hold jobs likely to be done by computers in the near future, including cooks, waiters, truck drivers, office workers, lawyers, and even teachers.[13] That these jobs can be automated is not saying that they should be. Ultimately, how we deal with the rest of the created world is our responsibility, in cooperation with God, and we must not deny that responsibility by passing it on to our own non-human creation. This becomes more difficult as we rely on technology that is increasingly complex. How many of us have been told that an error in our credit card or bank transactions was "made by the computer," or found an airline agent or shop clerk totally helpless because "the computer is down"? As we depend more and more on technology, we risk losing the skills that allow us to make decisions without that technology.

Until computers move beyond the functional, we will not see them as intelligent, as an image of ourselves or as a true co-creator. But how relational can a computer be? Science fiction presents AI in relational terms. Think of the lovable droids in *Star Wars*, the innocent David in *AI*, and more recently, Scarlett Johansson's sexy operating system voice in *Her* or Alicia Vikander's even sexier body in *Ex Machina*. In each of these films the plot revolves around the relationship between human and artificially intelligent characters. But what about in real life? Can we have an authentic relationship with a machine, given the state of our technology now or in the near future?

---

13. Muro, Maxim, and Whitten, "Automation and Artificial Intelligence," 5.

Some believe we will. They look to robots for companionship and even sex—in the words of Sherry Turkle, for relationship that is "safe and made to measure."[14] A woman who has sex with a robot does not risk pregnancy nor does a man who has sex with a robot risk impregnating. A robot can be programmed to give exactly the response we would like. Or turned off when one is not in the mood. But is this a real relationship? In *Humanae Vitae*, Pope Paul VI discusses sex wholly within the context of a love that is freely given, based in trust, exclusive, and "meant not only to survive the joys and sorrows of daily life, but also to grow, so that husband and wife become in a way one heart and one soul, and together attain their human fulfillment."[15] Here we have a number of stumbling blocks. Can a robot's love or affection be said to be freely given if it is programmed to always meet our needs? What does trust mean in a context where the machine can do no other than show caring behavior? And would a machine that does not grow old, sick, or face death share the "joys and sorrows of daily life"?

Setting sex aside, let us consider agape, or empathic love. Psychologist Simon Baron-Cohen defines empathy as "our ability to identify what someone else is thinking and feeling and to respond . . . with an appropriate emotion."[16] Compassion requires both recognition and response. Facial recognition software has made a beginning toward the recognition part, identifying expressions such as anger, delight, sadness, or disgust. IBM and Microsoft have both developed software that matches facial or vocal characteristics such as raised eyebrows or a raised voice to emotions in hopes that this could help machines identify customers' responses to a new product or allow them to calm an irate help line caller. But a review by five researchers of more than 1,000 studies has shown that the science underlying these technologies is deeply flawed, concluding that "the relationship between facial expression and emotion is nebulous, convoluted and far from universal."[17] Emotion detection systems are also prone to the biases of their programmers, mostly white or Asian men, thus making them far less reliable in recognizing the emotional states of women or persons from another culture. In 2007, the Transportation Security Administration introduced a program intended to help officers identify potential terrorists through their facial expressions and behavior. The program failed to identify a significant

14. Turkle, *Alone Together*, 66.

15. Pope Paul VI, *Humanae Vitae*, 329–46, 9.

16. Baron-Cohen, *The Science of Evil*, 16.

17. Telford, "'Emotion detection.'"

proportion of terrorists. Worse, a study by the American Civil Liberties Union concluded that because of embodied biases of its programmers its recommendations resulted in racial profiling.[18]

On the other end of the empathy continuum, computers can exhibit an emotional response—drooping ears or corners of the mouth on a robot, a sound like a laugh or a cry, a gaze from artificial eyes or a smile. Computers are far better at response than emotional recognition, but that tells us less about the machine than it does about our own human propensity to attribute emotion on the flimsiest of bases, not only to one another but to our pets, our stuffed animals, even our cars. Something as simple as the tilt of a robot's head has led humans to attribute a wide range of emotions such as warmth, attractiveness, and empathy.[19]

Hidden between recognition and response is the third requirement. We must respond with an authentic emotion. What does it mean to have an authentic emotion? Psychologist Jerome Kagan describes emotion as a four step process: 1) a change in brain activity due to a stimulus, 2) a perceived change in feeling that is sensory, 3) an appraisal of that feeling, and 4) a preparedness toward or display of a motor response.[20] As we have seen, computers are capable of a certain degree of numbers 1, 3, and 4. They can note a stimulus, albeit imperfectly, appraise that stimulus, and calculate an appropriate response.

It is the second step, a change in feeling that is sensory, a step that Kagan considers "critical," that computers do not have. This sensory basis for emotion can be seen in the linguistic roots of many of the terms we use to describe them: greed from grasping, fear from trembling, anger from grinding of the teeth.[21] We often feel strong physical responses, such as the rapid heartbeat, flushed face, and weak knees of anxiety, or the warm relaxation of love, before we have a cognitive recognition of what we are feeling. Consider, for example, how we involuntarily wince, and our skin becomes moist with sweat when we see pain being inflicted on another, or how our heart speeds up and adrenaline shoots into our bodies long before our consciousness registers fear. Indeed, it is precisely through the changes in our body that we first recognize an emotional response.

18. ACLU, "Bad Trip."

19. For examples of this tendency to attribute emotional states, see chapter 7 of Columbetti, *The Feeling Body*.

20. Kagan, *What are Emotions?*, 23.

21. Kagan, *What are Emotions?*, 42.

While we can turn the existence of this physical stage into information, we cannot digitalize the feeling itself. A computer does not feel
an emotion, it fakes it. It observes and then calculates an appropriate
response. What would it mean if a human being acted the same way,
calculating his or her responses rather than feeling them? According to
Baron-Cohen, one defining feature of a sociopath is an incomplete empathy circuit. The incompletion is not in the ability to see another or to
respond, but in the inability to feel. Without the physical ability to feel,
we cannot fully love. "Love made to measure" is not love. We don't have
authentically relational AI and probably never will. The relational robots
of film and fiction are precisely that: fiction.

The Real AI

So, what do we have? And how does it change the way we relate to one another? Google's DeepMind project has been going on now for more than ten
years.[22] It remains far from its goal of creating an artificial general intelligence
(AGI), a machine that can successfully complete any intellectual task that
a human can. Mustaffa Sulymann, one of the original founders and a member of the DeepMind Ethics Board, notes that the creation of an AGI is likely,
"very, very far away. We're decades and decades away from the kind of risks
that the board initially envisaged. We're putting in place a variety of other
mechanisms that focus on the near-term consequences."[23]

Those consequences are already with us. First, and foremost, AI is a military strategy. The US Defense Advanced Research Projects Agency (DARPA)
allocated over two billion dollars in 2018 as part of a five-year "Third Wave"
campaign aimed at developing machines that "can acquire human-like communication and reasoning capabilities."[24] These dollars are being spent to
develop programs in cybersecurity, detection of audio or video "deep fakes,"
facial recognition, and autonomous vehicles and weapons. Defense Department leaders expect these technologies "will change society and, ultimately,
the character of war."[25] The US is not alone in this development and is likely
behind China, which has spent billions on AI development in close

---

22. DeepMind began as a separate AI startup and was acquired by Google in 2014.

23. Shead, "DeepMind's Mysterious Ethics Board."

24. Harwell, "Defense Department pledges billions."

25. Harwell, "Defense Department pledges billions."

cooperation with corporations such as Alibaba and Huawei. According to investor and entrepreneur Peter Theil:

> A.I. is a military technology. Forget the sci-fi fantasy; what is powerful about actually existing A.I. is its application to relatively mundane tasks like computer vision and data analysis. Though less uncanny than Frankenstein's monster, these tools are nevertheless valuable to any army—to gain an intelligence advantage, for example, or to penetrate defenses in the relatively new theater of cyberwarfare, where we are already living amid the equivalent of a multinational shooting war.[26]

Most of us are unaware of these technologies as they come on line. One example is the launch in August 2019 of solar-powered high-altitude surveillance balloons over large portions of the Midwest. These balloons carry technology capable of tallying shipping containers or cars in a parking lot, even tracking and identifying any vehicle or person. Jay Stanley, senior policy analyst at the American Civil Liberties Union, notes their potential: "Even in tests, they're still collecting a lot of data on Americans: who's driving to the union house, the church, the mosque, the Alzheimer's clinic."[27]

Of course, the military is not the only entity using AI to collect our data. Adie Tomer of the Brookings Institute notes:

> Seemingly every human activity in the 21st century creates a data trail: business transactions, phone calls and text messages, turn-by-turn navigation. If you own a cellphone, simply moving from neighborhood to neighborhood creates a data trail as you jump from one cell tower to the next. Meanwhile, the equipment that constructs our buildings and infrastructure is now digitized, many of which can export data wirelessly. The computing industry also continues to innovate, creating ever-more processing power, storage capacity, and analytical software. We're simply awash in data and processing power.[28]

Programs to sift through and analyze this data represent much of what falls under the rubric of AI today. "When your video conference shifts the microphone to pick up the speaker's voice, when your smartphone automatically reroutes you around traffic, when your thermostat automatically lowers the

---

26. Thiel, "Good for Google, Bad for America."
27. Harris, "Pentagon testing."
28. Tomer, "Artificial intelligence."

air conditioning on a cool day—that's all AI in action."[29] Much of this AI is designed to make our lives simpler and more comfortable.

There have been few tools that we humans have not also found ways to use to gain power over others and AI is no different. We use the powers we have to collect, sift, and categorize data not just to understand but to manipulate. Consider Cambridge Analytica and the Russian troll factory, Internet Research Agency, both of which were successful in sowing seeds of distrust in the US electoral system and establishing groups and memes that sowed discord in the 2016 presidential election. On the domestic side, Facebook uses AI programs to decide what content you will see, which of your many "friends" posts, and what advertisements will appear on your news feeds. It also uses AI to identify pornography, hate speech, and fake accounts.

Once again, bias creeps into these programs. Worse, these programs foster and intensify biases in us. Software engineer Ben Dickson encapsulates the problem in a simple question. "What would happen if a news publisher printed a different copy of its newspaper for each of its subscribers?" This is, of course, what happens online. According to a 2018 Pew Research Center report, one in five US adults get their news primarily via social media while only 16 percent regularly read newspapers or other printed sources.[30] No two users see the same stories in their news feed. We live in increasingly separate bubbles, not just in terms of commentary, but even in terms of the facts we are told are true, a result of the business model of Facebook and other social media corporations, which use AI not to inform but to keep our eyeballs glued to the page and our mouse fingers clicking. As a result, we each live in a filtered bubble determined by an algorithm that gives us what it believes we want to see rather than what we might need to see. This has been a major factor in the political polarization we now see in the US, in which we exhibit less tolerance for opposing views and more vulnerability to fake news. The US is not alone in this. Social media has caused crises in elections in India and Brazil and fueled sectarian violence in Sri Lanka, Myanmar, and Hungary. It has played a major role in Britain's Brexit debacle.

A Question of Agency

Google's recent signature achievement, AlphaGo, does one thing. It plays Go. It plays Go really, really well, using novel strategies. Does that make

29. Tomer, "Artificial intelligence."
30. Shearer, "Social media ousts Newspapers."

it intelligent? No one programmed these strategies. AlphaGo was shown basic Go games and human strategies and then set to play itself thousands of times, learning from its mistakes. There are those who feel that anything that learns or makes choices has agency. My thermostat makes choices all day to turn the furnace on and off, but it hardly qualifies as an autonomous agent. But what about machines like AlphaGo that make choices unforeseen by their human programmers? This goes a step beyond the thermostat. Go champion Lee Sedol commented, "I thought AlphaGo was based on probability calculation and that it was merely a machine. But when I saw this move, I changed my mind. Surely, AlphaGo is creative."[31] What makes AlphaGo different from a human player, other than its being better? It comes down to a question of consciousness. AlphaGo is not aware of its choices; it is neither proud nor ashamed of them. It does not know it is playing Go, nor does it care. It is autonomous only in the sense that we are unaware of the ultimate consequences of its programming.

This failure to understand the ultimate consequences of our algorithms is an increasing problem. Not all unexpected results are as felicitous as the new strategies of AlphaGo. On March 18, 2018 Elaine Herzberg was the first pedestrian killed by an autonomous car. The car was unable to identify what she was as she pushed her bicycle with shopping bags hanging from the handlebars. Her death raises the question of how autonomous we want our machines to be. Since it's impossible for a programmer to anticipate every situation an autonomous vehicle might encounter, we'd like them to be able to learn from experience, as we do. But there are problems with this as well. A program that can change its own code is likely to do so in unforeseen ways. Computer scientist Ellen Ullman notes, "In some ways we've lost agency. When programs pass into code and code passes into algorithms and then algorithms start to create new algorithms, it gets farther and farther from human agency. Software is released into a code universe which no one can fully understand."[32]

This is not a new problem. MIT scientist Joseph Weizenbaum warned against such "incomprehensible programs" and our facile acceptance of their outputs back in 1976. Weizenbaum created a program called ELIZA which acted like a Rogerian psychologist, cleverly using the user's input as a template for further questions. Here is a short example:

(Patient): Men are all alike.

31. AlphaGo.

32. Smith, "Franken-algorithms."

48

(DOCTOR): IN WHAT WAY

(Patient): They're always bugging us about something or other.

(DOCTOR): CAN YOU THINK OF A SPECIFIC EXAMPLE

(Patient): Well, my boyfriend made me come here.

(DOCTOR): WHAT WOULD IT MEAN TO YOU IF YOU GOT SOME HELP

(Patient): Perhaps I could learn to get along with my mother.

(DOCTOR): TELL ME MORE ABOUT YOUR FAMILY

(Patient): My father is afraid of everybody.

(DOCTOR): WHAT ELSE COMES TO MIND WHEN YOU THINK OF YOUR FATHER

(Patient): Bullies.

(DOCTOR): DOES THAT HAVE ANYTHING TO DO WITH THE FACT THAT YOUR BOYFRIEND MADE YOU COME HERE[33]

Weizenbaum was shocked at people's responses to ELIZA. He did not expect users to believe the program was intelligent, but many did, spilling their problems to it, and some even claimed it passed the Turing Test, representing a machine that could converse on a human level.[34] Weizenbaum claimed this showed not only naivete about how computers work but also a distressing tendency to abdicate both our instrumental and moral agency to machines and to the institutions, the governments or corporations, that control them.

Weizenbaum feared such a relinquishment of human responsibility. This is particularly obvious in the context of the military. He writes:

> In modern warfare it is common for the soldier, say, the bomber pilot, to operate at an enormous psychological distance from his victims. He is not responsible for burned children because he never sees their village, his bombs, and certainly not the flaming children themselves . . . Not only does the most senior admiral of

33. Weizenbaum, *Computer Power and Human Reason*, 3–4.

34. ELIZA was probably the first of what we now call "chatbots." Many current chatbots are able to fool unsuspecting users for a time, especially today when they are loosed on circumscribed platforms such as Twitter or Instagram, but they are easily unmasked.

the United States Navy, in a rare moment of insight, perceive that he has become "a slave to these damned computers," that he cannot help but base his judgements on "what the computer says," but no human is responsible at all for the computer's output. The enormous computer systems in the Pentagon and their counterparts elsewhere in our culture have, in a very real sense, no authors.[35]

Remember, Weizenbaum was writing this almost half a century ago. His bomber pilot still had to fly over the village and take the action of launching a missile or dropping a bomb. Today's drone pilot sits in a bunker half a world away from his target, which he sees on a display that looks more like a video game than reality. It is all too easy to see his work as if it were a game. Fortunately, and unfortunately, the feeling of human responsibility is not that easily dismissed. While drone operators do not show the level of PTSD of soldiers on the ground, a significant number can be said to have sustained a "moral injury." Part of the problem is the immediate contrast between what the operator sees on his screen and the life he returns to when his shift is over. Retired pilot Jeff Bright reflected, "I'd literally just walked out on dropping bombs on the enemy, and 20 minutes later I'd get a text—can you pick up some milk on your way home?"[36] The bomber or drone operator is, at some level, still very much aware of being an autonomous agent, a part of the equation. The drone itself is not.

Agency and Introspection

What about machines that are not told how to make their choices, either by an operator or in their programming, and extend these choices into new realms? These are the dream of many who hope for an AGI. DeepMind moved in this direction in 2017, introducing Alpha Zero, a program that mastered three games—chess, shogi, and Go—"from scratch" given only the rules of each game. According to Alpha Zero's developers, this "demonstrates that a single algorithm can learn how to discover new knowledge in a range of settings, and potentially, any perfect information game . . . an important step towards our mission of creating general-purpose learning systems."[37] Surely this takes us one step closer to an AGI. But there is still a lot to overcome. First, note that Alpha Zero's learning techniques work for

35. Weizenbaum, *Computer Power and Human Reason,* 239.
36. Press, "The Wounds of the Drone Warrior."
37. AlphaGo.

"any perfect information game" but in most of life we have far from perfect information. Second, Alpha Zero did not take what it learned in one game and apply it to another. Each was viewed as a separate task.

A true AGI would need to synthesize across tasks, to make connections, to ruminate on what it has learned. Psychologist David Chalmers notes: "If you've just got an AI system that's modeling the world and not bringing itself into the equation" that is not enough. AGIs would need "introspective self-models, where they can know what's going on . . . from the first-person perspective."[38] Chalmers called this the "hard question" of consciousness. While he believes it is quite possible for a machine to make models or mental images of the world, we couple our mental images with both a knowledge that this image is mine and a feeling associated with that image. Psychologist Antonio Damasio, in his book *The Strange Order of Things*, underlines the necessity of these feelings, which he believes were selected for through evolution, noting that feelings, grounded in the body, are crucial to our ability to make decisions. We choose what to have for lunch not just through a rational process but by envisioning how each choice makes us feel. We choose what stocks to invest in the same way. We experience feelings about each investment path's possible outcomes that determine how we act, indeed give us the motivation to act at all. Damasio noted that patients whose brains were damaged in such a way that they could not feel emotion found it difficult to make even the most trivial of decisions.[39] Thus, full agency demands *telos*, that we have a purpose or reason to do what we do. We *want* to do something, and this wanting requires feelings grounded in bodily perception.

But bodies are inconvenient. They feel pain, they age, and they die. Many in the AI community look toward AI as a means of overcoming our bodies' flaws and ultimate mortality. Futurist and inventor Ray Kurzweil envisions downloading our brains into successive generations of computer technology:

> Up until now, our mortality was tied to the longevity of our hardware. When the hardware crashed, that was it. For many of our forebears, the hardware gradually deteriorated before it disintegrated . . . As we cross the divide to instantiate ourselves into our computational technology, our identity will be based on our evolving mind file. We will be software, not hardware . . .

38 Chalmers, "The Language of Mind."

39. Damasio, *The Strange Order of Things*.

> As software, our mortality will no longer be dependent on the survival of the computing circuitry . . . [as] we periodically port ourselves to the latest, evermore capable "personal" computer . . . Our immortality will be a matter of being sufficiently careful to make frequent backups.[40]

Kurzweil suggests we might achieve this new platform within the next twenty years. He is not the sole holder of this expectation, though he may be among the more optimistic in his timeline. In 2016 Elon Musk founded the corporation Neuralink, with the stated goal of "developing ultra-high bandwidth brain-machine interfaces to connect humans and computers."[41] While he touts this as a medical technology to help those with paralysis, he has also said he sees this as a first step toward merging humans and AI.

Kurzweil and Musk are only two adherents to a new movement called transhumanism, one that believes we should use all technological means to alter and improve the human condition. Most transhumanists believe that cybernetic immortality is consonant with the physical world. In that world all things are merely matter, or alternatively, merely information. This is a seductive worldview for the computer scientist who sees the world in terms of 0s and 1s. And to the scientific materialist, those parts of our being that seem the least material—consciousness, soul, or spirit—can be thought of as qualities that emerge as matter evolves or self-organizes into a sufficiently complex system.

But, so far, we have seen no evidence that this is true. We do not know what consciousness is, far less how to give it to a machine. We do know that it is precisely our ability to feel pain that gives rise to our moral values. Reward and punishment, pride and guilt are all a vital part of our learning to live together, to value certain acts over others, and to feel empathy for one another. Weizenbaum argues that people learn things machines cannot—for example, we understand natural language in the context of our experiences of love and trust, shame and pain, experiences a machine cannot have.[42] "What," he asks, "could it mean to speak of risk, courage, trust, endurance, and overcoming when one speaks of machines?"[43] No being without a human body can experience the pain and joy that underlie these things in quite the same way.

40. Kurzweil, *The Age of Spiritual Machines*, 280.

41. Neuralink.

42. Weizenbaum, *Computer Power and Human Reason*, 208–9.

43. Weizenbaum, *Computer Power and Human Reason*, 280.

So, it seems an AGI will not be a new neighbor with its own conscious-ness or agency, at least not until it acquires a humanlike body—one capable of feeling joy and pain and, yes, one that is as mortal as we are.

Conclusion: Being Neighbor

While AI is not yet giving us new robotic neighbors, computer technol-ogy has certainly enlarged the neighborhood. We have distance learning, prayers, posts, and photos sent to friends and distant family, ongoing conversations, research, and games with participants from all over the globe. And this can be marvelous. I have an ongoing email exchange with a graduate school friend who now lives in Vladivostok. I am part of an international group of researchers that is working together on a science and religion grant in Slovenia. My neighborhood is definitely bigger. But it's also less personal. We rarely see these neighbors face to face. We sometimes find there is much we do not know about the other.

What does it mean to truly be a neighbor? Karl Barth delineates four criteria. First, Barth says, we must look the other in the eye. Sight is our primary sense. To look the other in the eye is to apprehend the other at the most basic level. As the saying has it, "seeing is believing." I acknowl-edge the other as a separate being with a life and volition of his or her own when I look them in the eye. Barth's second criterion is to speak to and hear the other. Speech is the medium at which computers excel. How-ever, easy speech cuts both ways. The most pernicious shows how Barth's criteria are linked, as when speech is separated from the act of looking one another in the eye. Internet platforms lend themselves to anonymous speech that all too often denigrates into trolling or cyberbullying. Cyber-mobs form in minutes. Cyberbullying is increasingly prevalent among teens with over half claiming to have been a victim and an equal number admitting to being a victimizer.[44]

Barth's third and fourth criteria are also linked. We are to aid the other, and to do it gladly.[45] Computers can help us here. Communications professor Nicole Ellison has found that when people call for help from their Facebook network they generally get it, "whether they're looking for information, emo-tional support during a tough time, or even someone to help them with an

44. Cyber Bullying Statistics.

45. Barth, *Church Dogmatics* III/2, 250–53.

in-person favor, like lending them a book or driving them to the airport."[46] But this help has its limits. One teen notes: "Some people, like, help cheer you up online, but you don't really know them, so you can't really have a deep relationship."[47] A lack of tangible support from friends has contributed to a rise in loneliness among young people. Sociologist Jean Twenge best describes the connection: "Just as for happiness, the results are clear: screen activities are linked to more loneliness, and non-screen activities are linked to less loneliness."[48] It's easy to send likes or emojis, but these seem shallow compared to a warm hug, a physical helping hand.

The good Samaritan looked the beaten man in the eye, crossed over the road, and gave aid to him at his own expense. We can give and get information, thoughts and prayers, a kind word through cyberspace. Yet Barth reminds us that while aiding the other and speaking to and hearing the other are both crucial parts of authentic relationship, we still must look the other in the eye. The Samaritan was the first person passing along the road who truly saw the beaten man.

As Christians, we hold a very embodied faith, one based on the incarnation. God took on our mortal flesh in the person of Jesus and experienced the full spectrum of joy, empathy, pain, and finally, death. Barth insists on the centrality of Jesus as the only way to grasp both who God is and who we are meant to be. Thus, the incarnation is the key to both Christian theology and anthropology. It was through the taking on of a human body that God became fully present to humanity. By taking on our suffering and mortality, God entered into a fully authentic relationship with humankind. Though our bodies are the locus of pain and limitation, they are also necessary for our deepest expressions of love and solidarity. Embodied presence to one another is the best thing we have as human beings.

Mindless programs will overtake many of our currently mindless jobs. Deep learning will give us new correlations on which we will base an increasing number of decisions, some of them giving us new insights and aid, others leading to false premises and unjust actions. AI is already changing the ways we interact with one another and structure our society. But AI will not tell us how to respond to these changes. Only we, as we reflect on the lawyer's two questions—What must I do to be saved? and Who is my neighbor—will know how to respond, when to reach out using all of our

46. Beck, "Facebook."
47. Twenge, *iGen*, 73.
48. Twenge, *iGen*, 80.

technology, and when to step away from our screens, cross the road, and bind up another's wounds.

Bibliography

ACLU. "Bad Trip: Debunking the TSA's 'Behavior Detection' Program." February 2017. https://www.aclu.org/report/bad-trip-debunking-tsas-behavior-detection-program.

AlphaGo. https://deepmind.com/research/case-studies/alphago-the-story-so-far.

Baron-Cohen, Simon. *The Science of Evil*. New York: Basic, 2011.

Barth, Karl. *Church Dogmatics* III/1. Translated by J. W. Edwards, O. Bussey, and Harold Knight. Edinburgh: T. and T. Clark, 1958.

———. *Church Dogmatics* III/2. Translated by Harold Knight, G. W. Bromiley, J. K. S. Reid, and R. H. Fuller. Edinburgh: T. and T. Clark, 1960.

Beck, Julie. "Facebook: Where Friendships Go to Never Quite Die." *The Atlantic*, February 4, 2019. https://www.theatlantic.com/family/archive/2019/02/15-years-facebook-friendships-wont-die/581824/.

Chalmers, David. "The Language of Mind." *Edge,* August 8, 2019. https://www.edge.org/conversation/david_chalmers-the-language-of-mind.

Columbetti, Giovanna. *The Feeling Body: Affective Science Meets the Enactive Mind*. Cambridge, MA: MIT Press, 2013.

Cyber Bullying Statistics. http://www.bullyingstatistics.org/content/cyber-bullying-statistics.html.

Damasio, Antonio. *The Strange Order of Things: Life, Feeling, and the Making of Cultures*. New York: Penguin Random House, 2018.

Harris, Mark. "Pentagon testing mass surveillance balloons across the US." *The Guardian*, August 2, 2019. https://www.theguardian.com/us-news/2019/aug/02/pentagon-balloons-surveillance-midwest.

Harwell, Drew. "Defense Department pledges billions toward artificial intelligence research." *Washington Post*, September 7, 2018. https://www.washingtonpost.com/technology/2018/09/07/defense-department-pledges-billions-toward-artificial-intelligence-research/.

Hefner, Philip. *The Human Factor: Evolution, Culture, and Religion*. Minneapolis: Fortress, 1993.

Hehn, Johannes. "Zum Terminus 'Bild Gottes.'" In *Festschrift Eduard Sachau zum siebzigsten Geburtstag,* edited by Eduard Sachau, 36–52. Berlin: G. Reimer, 1915.

Herzfeld, Noreen. *In Our Image: Artificial Intelligence and the Human Spirit*. Minneapolis: Fortress, 2002.

Kagan, Jerome. *What are Emotions?* New Haven, CT: Yale University Press, 2007.

Kurzweil, Ray. *The Age of Spiritual Machines: When Computers Exceed Human Intelligence*. New York: Viking, 1999.

Muro, Mark, Robert Maxim, and Jacob Whitten. "Automation and Artificial Intelligence: How Machines are Affecting People and Places" Brooking Institution Report, January 24, 2019. https://www.brookings.edu/research/automation-and-artificial-intelligence-how-machines-affect-people-and-places/.

Neuralink. https://www.neuralink.com/.

Paul VI. *Humanae Vitae* (1968), §13. http://www.vatican.va/content/paul-vi/en/encyclicagols/documents/ht_p-vi_enc_25071968_humanae-vitae.html.

Press, Eyal. "The Wounds of the Drone Warrior." *New York Times*, June 13, 2018. https://www.nytimes.com/2018/06/13/magazine/veterans-ptsd-drone-warrior-wounds.html.

Shead, Sam. "DeepMind's Mysterious Ethics Board Will Reportedly 'Control' AGI If It's Ever Created." *Forbes*, March 14, 2019. https://www.forbes.com/sites/samshead/2019/03/14/deepminds-mysterious-ethics-board-will-reportedly-control-agi-if-its-ever-created/#1985658d52a9.

Shearer, Elisa. "Social media ousts newspapers in the U.S. as a news source." Pew Research, December 10, 2018. https://www.pewresearch.org/fact-tank/2018/12/10/social-media-outpaces-print-newspapers-in-the-u-s-as-a-news-source/.

Smith, Adam. "Franken-algorithms: the deadly consequences of unpredictable code." *The Guardian*, August 30, 2018. https://www.theguardian.com/technology/2018/aug/29/coding-algorithms-frankenalgos-program-danger.

Telford, Taylor. "'Emotion detection' AI is a $20 billion industry. New research says it can't do what it claims." *Washington Post*, July 31, 2019. https://www.washingtonpost.com/business/2019/07/31/emotion-detection-ai-is-billion-industry-new-research-says-it-cant-do-what-it-claims/.

Thiel, Peter. "Good for Google, Bad for America." *New York Times*, August 1, 2019. https://www.nytimes.com/2019/08/01/opinion/peter-thiel-google.html.

Tomer, Adie. "Artificial intelligence in America's digital city." Brookings Institute, July 30, 2019. https://www.brookings.edu/research/artificial-intelligence-in-americas-digital-city/.

Turkle, Sherry. *Alone Together: Why We Expect More from Technology and Less from Each Other*. New York: Basic, 2011.

Twenge, Jean. *iGen: Why Today's Super-Connected Kids Are Growing Up Less Rebellious, More Tolerant, Less Happy—and Completely Unprepared for Adulthood—and What That Means for the Rest of Us*. New York: Atria, 2017.

von Rad, Gerhard. *Genesis: A Commentary*. The Old Testament Library. Translated by John H. Marks. Philadelphia: Westminster, 1961.

Weizenbaum, Joseph. *Computer Power and Human Reason: From Judgment to Calculation*. San Francisco: Freeman, 1976.

Westermann, Claus. *Genesis 1–11: A Commentary*. Translated by John Scullion. Minneapolis: Augsburg, 1984.

Part II

How does social media in particular allow us to love our (digital) neighbor?

CHAPTER 3

When Religious Internet Memes about Religion Are Mean

Loving the Religious Other

HEIDI A. CAMPBELL

C hristians are called to love our neighbors as ourselves, a calling which has not changed in an age of digital media. Yet the culture created by social networks and digital communication makes this task increasingly a challenge. In our book *Networked Theology*, Stephen Garner and I explore three key questions regarding neighborliness in digital culture.[1] In reflecting on "who is my neighbor online," we explore the fact that while the Internet promotes trends towards both individualism and communalism, as Christians we are called to be communal beings. This challenges us to approach the Internet as a social network that calls us to connect with and relate to others in ways that model a Trinitarian outlook, seeing our lives as interconnected and influencing one another.

In reflecting on "where is my neighbor online," we consider how mediated environments like the Internet create new spaces of interaction that may suggest new rules for neighborliness. We conclude that while the Internet reshapes the realm of human experience, it is still a place, calling Christians to act in an affirming and relational way towards the other. The online-offline reality is new but not placeless, and our place-based faith requires us to negotiate betwixt and between this new context and the

1. Campbell and Garner, *Networked Theology*.

people found there. Finally, we explore, "how do we treat our neighbor online" by addressing the fact that although we find ourselves amidst new relationships and spaces of engagement, this does not negate the age-old call to treat our neighbor as ourselves. Being wrapped in media may create new social and communicative challenges in how we see and interact with others, but the call to show reciprocity and care in our engagements remains unchanged. Yet our initial exploration of the Christian responsibility of being neighbors online and the ways this informs how we see and treat others in digital culture fails to address an important emerging issue in an age of social media. That is, in what ways do the communication practices modeled in social media discourse seem to run counter to Christian narratives about neighborliness and encourage us to be uncaring or hostile to others online?

While social media offers us unique opportunities to connect with diverse individuals from across the globe, research has also found information overload can push us toward religious echo chambers. In the past decade, researchers have found individuals are more likely to use the Internet to seek out or create a digital tribe of like minds online, than to purposely build diverse online communities of those not like us.[2] In the 1990s the Internet was praised as a space that would encourage tolerance and diversity, as people met others from all occupations from around the globe.[3] Yet in the twenty-first century, researchers have noted people online are much more likely to gravitate towards those with shared interests and identities in order to manage the tensions and resounding cacophony of competing worldviews publicized and shared online.[4] Instead of encouraging us to engage with and love our neighbor online, there is a tendency for people online to remove themselves from spaces that force them to engage with others different from themselves.

Over the last six years, I have studied these trends in relation to an interesting area of digital culture: Internet memes. These are digital photographs or cartoon-like images or drawings that mix popular culture and media characters with playful or sarcastic statements about a variety of topics, including religion. Internet memes are frequently shared by people online via social media. This research explores the messages Internet memes share and promote about religion online. For example, popular

2. Brignall III and Van Valey, "An Online Community."

3. Gates, *The Road Ahead*.

4. Dutton et al., "Social Shaping of the Politics."

meme stock characters such as "Advice God," an image of God from Michelangelo's *Creation of Adam* placed on a triangular colored background, or "Religion Pigeon," an image of a pigeon presented on a similar background, are typically combined with text meant to mock a belief in God or question common Christian or religious practices and tenets. Approaching memes as cultural commentaries on popular understandings of religion in American culture has led to several interesting and concerning observations. This research shows Internet memes about religion circulated online predominately operate through a reliance on cultural tropes or stereotypes about religious individuals and their community, and so inadvertently spread religious bias online.

Internet memes about religion have a tendency to present religious beliefs in broad brushstrokes that highlight religious inconsistencies at best, and false, slanderous claims at their worst. These practices raise an interesting question in relation to our exploration of how we treat our neighbor online. What happens when digital media practices promote untruth or religious bias online? Or more specifically in the case of memes, what if the images we share via social media encourage us to *not* love our neighbor online?

In this chapter I explore these question by considering the role the Internet plays in promoting and spreading incivility towards religious individuals and cultures through the viral circulation of biased narratives about the religious other online. By studying the messages promoted by Internet memes about religion, we can investigate some of the common visual and textual discourses about religion in American culture commonly shared and circulated online. This also leads us to reflect on how we, as Christians, should respond to the ways the religious other, our digital neighbor, is framed online.

In order to focus this conversation, this chapter concentrates on how Islam and Muslims are frequently depicted online through Internet memes. By looking at a minority religion within American culture, and one that already faces frequent misunderstandings about its faith, we are able to highlight the bias Muslims have to engage with on a daily basis. Drawing evidence from two case studies of popular Internet memes about Islam also enables us to consider how social media and individuals online can easily spread, and thus promote, these problematic stereotypes. This helps us consider how sharing via social media may be an uncaring and unchristian act online if we are not self-aware and critical media readers and consumers in a digital age. Such meme messages can be seen as promoting religious microaggressions, small acts of violence committed by objectifying and mistreating the religious other. This requires critical ethical reflection on the fact that the act of not only creating but also sharing Internet memes can be seen as spreading religious violence through digital discourse.

How Internet Memes Communicate about Religion

As noted above, an Internet meme is a digital image from popular or Internet culture coupled with a humor-based slogan or caption to communicate common assumptions about a variety of events and topics, including religion. Memes get their name from Richard Dawkins, who defined them as ideas that spread virally throughout a society and become accepted, even though they may seem to make no logical sense.[5] He used this term to critique religion as a problematic meme, ergo the idea of meme has built within it the idea of critique and a negative view about religion.[6]

Due to the prevalence of meme-generator websites (e.g., the meme generators at imgflip.com, makeameme.org, etc.) that use popular meme images or allow individuals to download a photo and make a new version, it can take less than a minute to create a meme or a remixed version of an existing meme. This ease of production along with the ability to quickly post and share these images online have made memes highly popular on social media. These visual texts use different forms of humor to communicate common assumptions or beliefs individuals have about people of faith and the religious traditions they represent. Internet memes have become a unique and prolific genre of communication in digital culture. Take, for example, knowyourmeme.com, which has become the premier source for individuals who want to identify and learn about the origins and intentions behind many popular memes' "stock characters" and forms. Many of these memes are embedded with intricate backstories that influence the messages they communicate about different people and key ideas they seek to present.

With the rise in popularity of internet memes within digital culture today, scholars have begun to pay serious attention to how these digital artifacts based on humor convey messages related to religion. A study by Bellar et al. identified the different approaches in the construction, meaning

5. Dawkins, *The Selfish Gene.*
6. Campbell et al., "Responding to Meme-ing."

making, and circulation of religious Internet memes.[7] The authors found that memes largely use what is called "lived religion" to communicate. Lived religion is a particular understanding of religion coming out of Religious Studies, a concept that argues people's understanding of religion is based on how they seek to negotiate and live out religion in their daily lives, rather than following strict official codes of religious practice and dogma. David Hall (1997) described lived religion as the redefinition of the sacred in everyday American life, as religious beliefs and practices are seen as flexible, to be adapted to the lives of believers. The concept highlights a process by which people draw from religious teaching sources to make sense of their world. As Bellar, et al. argued, "Analyzing which cultural artifacts and ideas are used within religious-oriented memes—humorous or otherwise—reveals how various religious practitioners make sense of religion in their lives and how the public perceives faith in contemporary society."[8] This suggested that Internet memes typically present and seek to communicate or make sense of populist narratives about religion in everyday society. Internet memes about religion communicate commonly held cultural assumptions in succinct ways that are easily comprehended by readers, because they promote ideas that are easily recognizable to others. However, commonly held cultural beliefs may be based on stereotypes rather than truths, which can make the common a carrier of bias.

In addition, because it is almost impossible to track down the originator of most memes, it is very difficult to determine the original meaning or intent of these memes. Therefore, the meaning that lies behind and is communicated through memes is fluid and varies, regardless of whether one is the sharer, remixer, or viewer of the meme. This is also determined by an individual's experience or connection to the religion they are depicting in a meme. What may seem like a playful comment or funny image to one person may be seen in a very different way—such as hurtful or even cruel—to another.[9] On top of this, research conducted with my students surveying popular memes that portray not only Christianity, but Islam, Judaism, Hinduism, and Buddhism online has found that internet memes about religion are much more likely to be critical of religion, rather than supportive.[10] It has also shown that the playful character of memes as on-

7. Bellar et al., "Reading Religion in Internet Memes."
8. Bellar et al., "Reading Religion in Internet Memes."
9. Aguilar et al., "Communicating Mixed Messages."
10. Campbell et al., "Responding to Meme-ing."

line image-based humor can often distract audiences from hurtful and even hate-filled messages about religion, especially when religious groups respond to social or political messages or events.[11] This means Internet memes have a tendency to highlight negative views about various faith communities and their followers. As a result, individuals who are part of communities outside the dominant religious or social group in a culture are often "othered" or objectified.

Investigating Religious Stereotypes in Internet Meme Culture

Digital media, an ever-changing presence in today's society, affects people's lives through content such as Internet memes and the discourse surrounding them. Memes have the potential to spark discussion over sensitive issues—like religion, race, and minority cultures—through the implicit and explicit messages they convey. When the messages of memes criticize beliefs about Islam and the identity of its followers, they often conflate the ideas of religion and race. In other words, Internet memes often address how those outside a religious group tend to equate them with a single identity, racial, or cultural group.

Using stereotypes as a cultural shorthand to characterize the identity of minority groups is not a new phenomenon. Scholars concerned about communication ethics and intercultural communication have written extensively about how media employ stereotypes to frame minority groups not widely familiar in a culture, which can influence how individuals treat and see one another.[12] Scholars have also found people are more likely to activate social stereotypes associated with cultures that are in the minority and that they are unfamiliar with.[13] In an era of digital media that enables individuals to easily create and present stereotypes through new communication forms and spread these ideas even more quickly and widely than was possible with other generations of media, concerns are being raised about what influence digital media may have relative to reinforcing such problematic cultural messages.

---

11. Campbell et al., "The Dissonance of 'Civil' Religion."

12. Seiter, "Stereotypes and the Media."

13. Hogg and Reid, "Social Identity."

Initial research exploring how religion is discussed through Internet memes found memes are often framed in the language of the outsider.[14] Memes about religion often adopt the voice or stance of those outside the religious community represented, so memes can be perceived to be produced by community outsiders. This study conducted with my graduate students at Texas A&M University also found memes commonly deal in the currency of stereotyping. In other words, memes use images and text that promote assumptions about those outside a specific religious community to frame their subjects. This means memes function by highlighting broad outsider assertions about many minority religious groups, specifically framing their assumptions about their religious beliefs and practices.[15] This occurs because meme narratives cannot easily deal with nuance or diversity of interpretations within these short texts accompanying a single image.

How Islam Is Framed in Internet Memes

Complications can arise because narratives about religious beliefs often require their audiences to have specialized knowledge about the specific faith tradition involved in order to fully comprehend punch lines or claims. Therefore, memes "feature reductionist or essentialized understandings of religion and employ a limited range of popular assumptions or metanarratives about religion in order to communicate to a broad audience."[16] This means memes use oversimplified characterizations of religious practices and beliefs in order to communicate within this succinct medium. This can lead to problematic narratives, especially in how popular Internet memes depict Islam.

To focus our discussion, this chapter provides insights from a case study exploring Muslim-oriented internet memes and the stereotypes they spotlight. This study highlights dominant stereotypes associated with internet memes focused on Muslim beliefs and practices drawn from a large cross-religion comparative study of almost 500 memes depicting Judaism, Hinduism, Catholicism, Mormonism, and Islam. The aim of this study was to gather memes that exemplify the ways in which meme creators use memetic discourse to communicate common assumptions and messages about religious communities from the dominant world religions. Here I

14. Bellar et al., "Reading Religion in Internet Memes."
15. Bellar et al., "Reading Religion in Internet Memes."
16. Bellar et al., "Reading Religion in Internet Memes," 24.

share findings about the three common narratives memes from this study communicate about Muslims and the implications of circulating such narratives online. This case study shows that Internet memes do offer a sort of cultural shorthand, presenting common images and beliefs in a playful way so diverse audiences can easily read them. Yet behind the humor often lie problematic stereotypes and extremist framings of Islam that do not offer a balanced or truthful understanding of this religious community.

This study began with a collaborative research project conducted by undergraduate students taking a course on religious communication I taught at Texas A&M University in the fall of 2017. Students were instructed to research a religion other than their own and identify a prevalent stereotype being associated with a specific belief or practice of that religion through the use of Internet memes. From this work, a collective sample of approximately 290 memes was identified. Admittedly, this selective sample of memes prevents us from making broad claims about the representative nature of the sample and analysis. However, by gathering memes posted online during a specified period of time and found on the top page of Google Image searches for specified themes, we were able to assess how religion is presented in common, viral memes. These findings were documented in individual research diary blogs at http://comm48otamu.blogspot.com/.

Using this initial work, a team conducted further research on religious stereotypes in meme culture. Recurring themes and stereotypes were documented for each religion, including information on whether the stereotype referred to a belief or practice. Following this initial review, a Google Image search for each religion was conducted using search phrases such as "Muslim memes," "Islamic memes," etc., to verify the accuracy of initial findings. From this a final sample of ninety meme images on Islam was collected, in which the top three stereotypes for this religion were identified and individually searched using Google Images in order to ascertain levels of prevalence for each stereotype and help further identify the common messages being conveyed about religious communities through the online meme culture. This final sample was then analyzed and coded accordingly based on insider or outsider perspective, positive-affirming or critical-negative views, and Aguilar et al.'s framing categories. Meme frame definitions were extended in this research to include the notion of stereotypes and religion—i.e., mocking religion was expanded to include memes used to mock a certain stereotype based on religious beliefs or practices.[17] The combined classification of these criteria led to the development of several subcategories and surfaced several subthemes, findings for which are discussed below.

Three dominant assumptions about the nature of Islam as a religion were identified through the memes collected in this study. These included: (1) Islam is a religion of contradictions, promoting violence over being a religion of peace; (2) all Muslim women are culturally oppressed; and (3) Islam is an anti-American religious culture and problematic in terms of the politics it represents or encourages. Below I further describe and explain these narratives promoted by the analyzed memes and the problematic they create as they frame Islam in a biased way and shame Muslims as the religious other.

Muslims as Angry Arabs, Promoting Violence over Being a Religion of Peace

First, the overwhelming majority of memes in this study communicated a critical position towards Islam, especially mocking the notion that Islam describes itself as a religion of peace.

Our search for and identification of prominent memes via Google Images using the phrase "Islam memes" found many of these particular memes seemed to be created by outsiders commenting on Islamic beliefs and were overtly critical-negative. One example shows a man pointing a gun, with an image captioned, "What part of religion of peace do you not understand?" This meme is categorized as negative because it presents Islam as a religion not of peace but violence—the ostensibly Muslim man points the gun at the viewer of the meme. The most dominant religious frame in this sample was the mocking-religion frame. Another example shows a divided-picture meme, the top half showing a "Muslim" man holding an AK-47 and the caption, "How we see Muslims." In the bottom picture, the AK-47 is now seen from a first-person perspective aiming at other people in the background. The caption on this half reads, "How Muslims see us." Therefore, these memes criticizing the idea that Islam could be seen as peaceful did so by equating all Muslims as associated with or supporters of the Islamic State, or ISIS. This was done in order to challenge the idea of Islam supporting peace, instead insinuating it is inherently violent in its practices. This depiction is very common in other media narratives about Islam. Graeme Wood stated

17. Aguilar et al., "Communicating Mixed Messages."

in his article "What ISIS Really Wants" that the prevalence of news coverage of the Islamic State and the common identification of ISIS as a religiously focused political group in the news strengthen this association. He also said this stereotype is strengthened as media describe ISIS's political actions and agenda as religious: "The religion preached by its most ardent followers derives from coherent and even learned interpretations of Islam."[18]

The studied memes also speak overwhelmingly in voice of the expert outside the Muslim community who is best able to describe Arabs and Muslim culture. This is a classic trait of "orientialism" discussed by Edward Said that suggests narratives of the Muslim world often portray Western observers as the ones best able to define the identity of Arabs and Muslims.

Thus, by using images of Muslims acting violently and text that affirms this as part of their religious tradition, these memes oversimplify and skew Islamic teaching about jihad as a core basis of their religion. These images also assert that all Muslims are Arabs, a demographic falsehood in the USA and other parts of the world. So these memes falsely associate all Muslims and their practice with violence. This gives no space for a true discussion or depiction of Muslims and their doctrine of peace, such as the idea that the word *salaam,* or peace, in Arabic has the same root as the word *Islam.* These memes about Muslims should be viewed as always possessing values that run contrary to majority religions such as Christianity.

Islam Is Abusive to Women, as All Muslim Women Are Culturally and Religiously Oppressed

The second most common narrative expressed by memes in our study sample communicates the idea that Muslim women should be viewed as oppressed through their religion, and that Muslim men will abuse them. For example, one meme depicts a woman acting like a puppet controlled by a Muslim man, who is manipulating her and speaking on her behalf while defending her manner of dress against a white man's disapproval by saying, "Listen, you arrogant white man, when you tell us to remove our burkas, you are oppressing women." The meme portrays a very negative image, of a woman not allowed to speak for herself. It suggests that this is what Islam advocates, for women to be controlled by men and to be treated without any freedom in their society. This suggests Islam advocates and supports oppression and inequality, two values highly antithetical to Western,

18. Wood, "What ISIS Really Wants," 1.

American culture. Other memes supporting this narrative stress that Islam is to be mocked because of these purported core cultural standards and practices it represents. One meme displaying the mocking-religion frame shows a picture of a woman dressed in a *hijab*; the caption reads, "Me? Oppressed? Look at all the stuff my husband lets me do." In this meme, the woman stands there doing nothing, staring with blank eyes through her burqa. Laced with sarcasm, the meme mocks those who might assert that Islam does not oppress women. These memes all depict women as silent, subservient, and passive, and any men depicted appeared to affirm rather than stand against the stereotype.

Again, this is not a new stereotype, but one often associated with Muslim communities. Myra MacDonald in "Muslim Women and the Veil" wrote about the perceived significance of the Muslim woman's veil and how it is represented in Western culture. She suggested, "'The veil' becomes an all-encompassing symbol of repression, and in its dominant association with Islam (with equivalent Jewish, Christian, or Hindu practices written out of the script) reinforces the monocular representation of that religion."[19] This shows these memes reinforce popular stereotypes from outsiders commenting on Islam as a flawed religion because of its perceived inequality towards women. Memes that show women wearing similarly restrictive clothing commonly use the word *oppressed/oppression* in their associated text. However, such memes offer a very one-sided view of veiling within Islamic cultures. They also fail to offer an opening to discuss alternative narratives of the religious significance many Muslim women, especially in Western culture, associate with the veil as they actively choose to wear it for moral reasons. In this way, such memes silence the potential for dialogue and further objectify and support the oppression of those they seek to critique.

Islam Is Anti-American, so Muslims Are Violent towards USA Cultural-Religious Beliefs

Third, many of the memes in this study stressed the narrative that Islam is anti-American. This is done by depicting strong tensions between the United States and Muslim cultures. Specifically, Islam is portrayed as a backward religion that promotes beliefs and practices attacking American democratic values. This is interesting because here we see a problematic mixing of

19. MacDonald, "Muslim Women and the Veil," 8.

political and religious narratives that highlights contradiction of the religious outsider as expert voice. In memes showing Muslims as terrorists, we see Islam is critiqued for mixing politics with religion. Yet in these same memes, we see that the Islamic religious beliefs expressed uphold similar understandings of American political and cultural values as standards.

Memes in the Google Image sample presenting this narrative often depicted President Donald Trump, Hilary Clinton, or former President Barack Obama with humorous captions meant to suggest they represented each of these individual's specific views on Islam and Muslims. Again, we noted all these memes seemed to speak in the voice of those outside the Muslim community and portray highly critical-negative views of Islam as a religion. One such meme depicts Obama on a game show trying to guess a phrase, such as *Wheel of Fortune.* The letters are meant to spell "Islamic Terrorism." Obama states, "Gee, Pat, I don't have a clue . . . Workplace violence? Uh, armed insurgency? Can I buy a vowel?" This meme portrays Obama as unwilling to associate Islam with terrorism and criticizes him for not naming it. Such memes use a frame that mocks the reality of what Islam is seen to culturally and religiously represent. Another meme, also using a photo of Obama, shares the caption, "Republicans want to give Muslim Refugees a Religious Test . . . it's shameful." The next part of the meme shows ISIS members shooting at hostages and bears the caption, "Muslims give Christians a Religious Test. Not a word from Obama." This meme implies again that Obama does not correctly see or understand Islam and its violent tendencies. Again, it also equates all Islam with radical factions of Islam. It further portrays Obama as passive and not willing to intervene when American religious or cultural values are at stake. In other words, these memes present Islam as not only problematic in terms of its core cultural identity, they stress that Islam is always political, which shapes its religious practices and beliefs.

Many of these memes could be also described as promoting Islamophobia, or an "exaggerated fear, hatred, and hostility toward Islam and Muslims that is perpetuated by negative stereotypes."[20] Islamophobia is supported and justified by these memes, which emphasize Islam as a religion that runs counter not only to American Christianity but also to the very cultural values on which the USA is founded. Thus, to be a true American is to critique or even hate Muslims.

20. Gallup, *Islamophobia.*

The Problem with Muslim Memes

This brief study highlights just some of the key assertions communicated by common or popular Internet memes about Islam circulating and found online. Overall, they promote not only negative framing of Muslims, but advocate the idea that Islam should be viewed and responded to in a biased light. However, as noted above, stereotypes presenting Islam as violent, oppressive to women, and anti-American are not new narratives or narratives that can be uniquely associated with meme messages about Islam. Indeed, scholars have noted such public stereotypes and associations have become increasingly common in media post 9/11, but date back decades, if not centuries, before these attacks.[21] What this research echoes is the fact that the most visible messages being circulated online are based on already biased framings of Islam and, unfortunately, simply extend and propagate these problematic narratives.

Overwhelmingly, Internet memes communicate in the voice of the religious outsider, spotlighting perceived problematic practices and values noted in other oversimplified framings of the Islamic religion. This is a classic strategy, noted by scholars and highlighted by popular media tendencies towards orientalism in the framing of Islam, or what I describe as the other-ing of religious minorities. The external Western expert takes away the voice of the faith community, their ability to speak for themselves and respond to broad, biased cultural stereotypes. While this study did identify some memes that suggested more nuanced framings of Islam are possible online, such as memes that stress the racial and ethnic diversity found within Muslim communities, overall these were much less prevalent in the sample. This means that while the voice of religious insiders seeking to promote alternative narratives and discredit stereotypes can be found, such memes are less visible in broad, general searches of Muslim memes online.[22]

This means that unless we recognize that memes about religion tend to speak in the voice of community outsiders, are driven by stereotypes, and communicate oversimplified narratives about religion, we will not recognize how they tend to skew the beliefs and identities of those they seek to represent. Memes can easily be misinterpreted, because they rely on humor such as irony or sarcasm to make their point, a characteristic that

21. Abu-Nimer and Hilal, "Combatting Global Stereotypes."
22. Campbell et al., "Responding to Meme-ing."

can disarm our critical reading of them. By also employing the rhetoric of stereotypes to frame aspects of religion, they function on the basis of a cultural shorthand that does not and cannot show the whole. An ability to recognize how memes about religion function is crucial if we are to recognize what they are and the limits of their truth telling. In his 2013 article "Hacking the Social," Milner argued that digital culture often reinforces oppressive ideologies: "[Posters] operate in an environment where racial stereotypes were an understood and largely unchallenged assumption."[23] Our findings unfortunately echoed this assertion, showing that memes tend to convey oppressive messages and beliefs about others online. This represents a challenge to how we are to respond to the question posed at the beginning of this chapter: What do we do when social media discourse encourages us not to love our neighbor online?

Responding to the Memeing of the Religious Other as a Neighbor Online

In this chapter I have argued that because Internet memes are humorous artifacts and are easily created and spread virally through social media, they tend to fly under our radar relative to the impact they can have online. The result is that meme messages, which often function on the basis of religious stereotypes, can easily become purveyors of hostile and unkind discourse in contemporary digital culture. This is a phenomenon in need of more critical Christian reflection. So, how should we respond to the meme-ing of the religious other online? I believe this research on religious Internet memes presents us with several important observations and potential action steps in need of further consideration.

First, because memes shared online often convey compact messages about complex subjects, they often point to the need for more detailed reflection and conversations that unpack the cultural assumptions about religion they communicate. As Yoon argued, memes are important because "[they] have the potential to open a new door for reflection" by presenting and framing seemingly lofty concepts or arguments for pop culture in ways that make them more easily accessible to the average person.[24] However, as this study shows, important information and substance can be lost in the meme translation process. In addition to discussing

23. Milner, "Hacking the Social," 39.
24. Yoon, "Why Is It Not Just a Joke?," 117.

what the obvious content of the meme seeks to communicate, memes about religious others should be treated as a space for active conversation and not just passive sharing. Yoon, for example, said it is important to analyze the power relations displayed by memes, as well as the potential emotional reactions they can generate from different audiences. Sharing memes online is easy, but transforming them into tools of reflection and learning is not. This requires reflection on what makes them humorous or how a given individual or topic is framed by the meme and the hidden assumption behind these. We should see memes as not just depictions of popular notions about the religious other, but as opportunities to study the deeper meanings of the messages they communicate.

Second, I believe that as Christians we are called to be critical consumers of digital content, not just passive audiences. I believe Christians are called to be truth-tellers and function online with discernment. In the case of Internet memes, this means when a meme comes across our social media feed about someone, especially the religious outsider, we need to pause and consider what this depiction seeks to represent, and does its presence on my feed or my potential sharing of it require action on my part. As suggested above, this requires a careful reading where one needs to ask important context-specific questions in order to clearly expose not only the messages memes communicate, but their underlying cultural assumptions and biases. Such questions include:

- *What message does the digital image in the meme portray or represent?*

- *How do the texts of the meme shape its meaning and express certain assumptions?*

- *In what ways should I respond to this meme? How can I do so in way that resists spreading religious biases or othering?*

If we as individuals online learn to ask these types of questions when considering Internet memes, we will help originators/sharers/viewers develop improved critical thinking skills and enable them to interrogate the messages spread about religion within digital culture. I suggest memes can be used as teachable moments to expose bias and stereotypes or create conversations that call prejudice into question. I believe engagement with memes can be shaped as moments of reflection that can move us toward actions demonstrating increased care, respect, and valuing for people's differences, even when it comes to differences in faith and worldview.

Matthew Kaemingk in *Christian Hospitality and Muslim Immigration in an Age of Fear* argued that Christianity has long bought into the "Clash of Civilization" thesis, in which Islam as a culture and religion is framed in a negative light. [25] The clash occurs as "the West," where Christianity is central, is presented as representing pure good, in contrast to Islam as representative of pure evil since it stands against Western values and norms. This framing creates an antagonistic relationship between the West/Christianity and Islam and is used to justify negative framings and objectification of Islam in public discourse. This allows and even encourages Westerners to see Muslims as less than or nonhumans, a tendency shown in previous research about how Islam is framed in popular media, a tendency also revealed in the findings of this study. This vilifying and scapegoating of Islam, Kaemingk suggested, runs counter to the Christian call to hospitality and treating the stranger in our midst with respect and care. It also pushes against Jesus' call to be neighbors to those who are different from us.

Similarly, Garner and I suggest that digital culture should not be a place of exception in how we treat our online neighbors. Rather, the challenge faced by Christians and the church in online culture is to:

> call for a recognition of neighbors and neighborhood that demands a radical acknowledgement of the humanity present in those we encounter in both physical and virtual worlds. It also refuses to remove the presence of God from those virtual neighborhoods and treats our physical and virtual neighbors with a love and justice . . .[26]

Overall, this chapter has sought to argue that Internet memes about religion, as they currently stand, often act as religious microaggressions, acts of unkindness against other religions. This supports problematic narratives such as the clash-of-civilization thesis, that justify and excuse ideological violence and inhospitality to religious minorities in our culture. I believe if Internet memes are passively engaged and left unchecked, they often, by default, communicate and spread messages that can promote religious stereotypes. As a result, they act as microaggressions by objectifying the religious other. Yet in digital culture, just as we are urged in Scripture, Christians are called to acts of care that show value to the strangers/neighbors amongst us. Therefore, I suggest those who engage in social media have a responsibility to actively read and analyze the roots of problematic

25. Kaemingk, *Christian Hospitality and Muslim Immigration.*
26. Campbell and Garner, *Networked Theology,* 95.

narratives circulated by Internet memes. By doing so, we can create a new conversational space online, which can transform memes into moments of religious understanding and reciprocity.

Bibliography

Abu-Nimer, Mohammed, and Maha Hilal. "Combatting Global Stereotypes of Islam and Muslims: Strategies and Interventions for Mutual Understanding." In *The State of Social Progress of Islamic Societies (International Handbooks of Quality-of-Life)*, edited by Habib Tiliouine and Richard Estes, 623–41. New York: Springer, 2016.

Aguilar, Gabrielle, Heidi Campbell, Mariah Stanley, and Ellen Taylor. "Communicating Mixed Messages about Religion through Internet Memes." *Information, Communication, & Society* 20.10 (2017) 1458–1520.

Bellar, Wendi, Heidi Campbell., Kyong Cho, Andrea Terry, Ruth Tsuria, Aya Yadlin-Segal, and Jordan Zeimer. "Reading Religion in Internet Memes." *Journal of Religion, Media and Digital Culture* 2.2 (2013). https://www.jrmdc.com/journal/article/view/13.

Brignall, Thomas, III, and Thomas L. Van Valey. "An Online Community as a New Tribalism: The World of Warcraft." Paper presented at 40th Annual Hawaii International Conference on System Sciences (HICSS '07), Waikoloa, HI, 2007. doi:10.1109/HICSS.2007.71.

Campbell, Heidi. "Communicating about Faith in a Mean 'Meme' World: Responding to Religious Uncivil Discourse in Digital Culture." Paper presented at Religious Communication Association, Dallas, 2017.

———, Katherine Arrezndo, Katie Dundas, and Cody Wolf. "The Dissonance of 'Civil' Religion in Religious-Political Memetic Discourse During the 2016 Presidential Elections." *Social Media+Society* 4.10 (April 2018). doi:10.1177/2056305118782678.

———, and Stephen Garner. *Networked Theology*. Grand Rapids: Baker Academic, 2016.

———, Lane Joiner, and Samantha Lawrence. "Responding to the Meme-ing of the Religious Other." *Journal of Religion and Communication* 14.2 (2018) 27–42.

———, Morgan Knobloch, and Danielle Gonzalez. *Meme-ing Muslims: Study on How Islam, Race and Religion are Framed by Internet Memes*. Religious (In)Tolerance and Diversity in Digital Media & Culture Seminar, Texas A&M University, College Station, TX. https://digitalreligion.tamu.edu/blog/tue-09042018-1722/mememing-muslims-study-how-islam-race-and-religion-are-framed-internet-memes.

Dawkins, Richard. *The Selfish Gene*. Oxford: Oxford University Press, 1976.

Dutton, William, Bianca Reisdorf, Elizabeth Dubois, and Grant Blank. "Social Shaping of the Politics of Internet Search and Networking: Moving Beyond Filter Bubbles, Echo Chambers, and Fake News." Quello Center Working Paper No. 2944191, March 31, 2017. https://ssrn.com/abstract=2944191 or http://dx.doi.org/10.2139/ssrn.2944191.

Gallup. *Islamophobia: Understanding Anti-Muslim Sentiment in the West.* http://news.gallup.com/poll/157082/islamophobia-understanding-anti-muslim-sentiment-west.aspx.

Gates, Bill. *The Road Ahead.* New York: Viking, 1995.

Hall, David. *Lived Religion in America: Toward a History of Practice.* Princeton, NJ: Princeton University Press, 1997.

Hogg, Michael, and Scott A. Reid. "Social Identity, Self-categorization, and the Communication of Group Norms." *Communication Theory* 16.1(2006) 7–30.

Joiner, Lane, and Samantha Lawrence. "Religious Stereotypes in Internet Meme Culture." Paper presented during Student Research Week, Texas A&M University, College Station, TX, 2018.

Kaemingk, Matthew. *Christian Hospitality and Muslim Immigration in an Age of Fear.* Grand Rapids: Eerdmans, 2018.

MacDonald, Myra. "Muslim Women and the Veil." *Feminist Media Studies* 6.1 (2006). doi:10.1080/14680770500471004.

Milner, Ryan. "Hacking the Social: Internet Memes, Identity Antagonism, and the Logic of Lulz." *The Fibreculture Journal* 22 (2013). http://twentytwo.fibreculturejournal. org/fcj-156-hacking-the-social-internet-memes-identity-antagonism-and-the-logic-of-lulz/.

Seiter, Ellen. "Stereotypes and the Media: A Re-Evaluation." Journal of Communication 36.2 (1986) 14–26.

Shifman, Limor. *Memes in Digital Culture.* Cambridge, MA: MIT Press, 2013.

Wood, Graeme. "What ISIS Really Wants." *The Atlantic,* March 2015. https://www. theatlantic.com/magazine/archive/2015/03/what-isis-really-wants/384980/.

Yoon, Ingeon. "Why Is It Not Just a Joke? Analysis of Internet Memes Associated with Racism and Hidden Ideology of Colorblindness." *Journal of Cultural Research in Art Education* 33 (2016) 93–123. https://search.proquest.com/openview/f215879d26fbd 6eca4f29e350c75e897/1?pq-origsite=gscholar&cbl=2031815.

CHAPTER 4

Data, Discernment, & Duty

Illuminating Engagement in the Internet of Things

PAULINE HOPE CHEONG

One of the key paradoxes of today's increasingly mediated environ-ments in regions where digital computing is prevalent is the (in)vis-ibility of media. As contemporary technological innovations are embedded in our "smart" homes, schools, and churches, sensors in our neighborhoods, and even microchipped in ourselves, the nature of digital connectivity has changed. This "Internet of Things" (IoT) or the dense global ecosystem of connected devices and applications, is closely associated and sustained by "Big Data"—vast troves of structured, semi-structured, and unstructured data that are transferrable over digital networks and analyzed computa-tionally with real-time collection, tracking, and predictive analyses.[1] As the Internet is now metaphorically and literally woven into the fabric of daily life, datafication or the "ability to render into data many aspects of the world that have never been quantified before" has implications for everyday operations, including religious life.[2]

Forecasts of an epochal growth in worldwide data point to the criti-cal importance of datafication for automation, machine learning, and ar-tificial intelligent (AI) systems.[3] Data-enabled interactions are expected to

1. Chen, Mao, and Liu, "Big Data," 171.
2. Cukier and Mayer-Schoenberger, "The Rise of Big Data," 29.
3. Anderson and Rainie, *The Future of Big Data.*

increase multifold as an average connected person is projected to interact with connected devices nearly 4,800 times per day, or one interaction every eighteen seconds.[4] As we become increasingly accustomed to deploying artificial intelligence and Big Data in our habitual experiences, it has even been proposed that the modern human species Homo sapiens will evolve into an upgraded breed of superhuman: "Homo Deus."[5] As such and in response to the conference, Techno-sapiens in a networked era, that catalyzed this chapter, it is significant to consider how datafication forms the socio-technical context within which Christian communities are situated and missional life is expressed.

To provide a portal for understanding present-day datafication, this chapter will first highlight two major points regarding datafication by drawing upon church history and technology studies. Akin to extreme scenarios accompanying prior technological innovations, both utopic and dystopic visions of datafication have been presented. Enthusiasm for data-driven innovations have been embraced by religious advocates. On the other end, critiques toward a data approach to religion have been voiced concerning its biased and unjust nature. The front section of the chapter will then point to the need to consider a dialectical perspective in religious datafication as bigger data streams intertwine with concurrent tensions in the development of religious identity, community, and authority today.[6]

The next section will unpack and illustrate multiple dialectics of datafication at play as it pertains to key trends in contemporary religiously related practices. As IoT becomes more critical, yet more unobtrusive and inconspicuous to us, the aim here is to raise questions and spur collective reflection about the profound and enduring tensions that datafication poses for the norms and practices of missional engagement, particularly for churches today. As I approach this topic as a communication scholar drawing upon interdisciplinary perspectives, it resounds with me strongly how our duty to love our neighbors requires our interdisciplinary collaboration and discernment in digitally embedded socio-technological systems.

---

4. Reinsel, Gantz, and Rydning, "Data Age 2025."

5. Harari, *Homo Deus*.

6. See Cheong and Arasa, "Religion," and Cheong and Ess, "Introduction."

Religious datafication: recognizing plural historical and contemporary pulses

Although the term *Big Data* has recently drawn popular attention, it is abstract and amorphous, underlying the need for understanding datafication in specific settings, including in the religious context. Echoing the emergence of new technology over the years, datafication with IoT has drawn popular attention with dominant views skewed toward utopic and dystopic sentiments in religious circles and beyond.

Contrary to common perceptions of secularization, deepening schisms between technology and religion, there are historical precedents and current examples of taking a data approach to religion by Christ followers. As I have explicated elsewhere, datafication today has a history in religious hosts and contexts: "Over the centuries, religious personnel have advocated for the quantification of different forms of socio-demographic, behavioral and economic data via numeric record keeping and accounting procedures for statistical analyses and strategic planning."[7] On the other extreme, in line with dystopic projections and prior suspicions of new media to elevate human society, critiques have been cast upon forms of datafication that are influenced by narrow partisan interests, church leadership, and goals. A discussion of the parallels between past and present cases can illuminate understandings of the continuities and complexities of taking a data approach to religion.

First, enthusiasm toward a functionalist approach to church data has been expressed over the years. Religious advocates have pressed for the tracking and analysis of church behavioral data prior to the development of digital media.[8] Church leaders have stressed the importance of adopting the latest technologies (e.g. from the then novel use of spreadsheets to modern management practices) for a careful accounting of church resources. The importance of classification and data archival was evident in the laying down of requirements for almost all the dioceses in the US Protestant Episcopal Church to compile statistics related to church activities and financial and sociodemographic data into formal church records by 1860.[9] Moreover, pedagogy related to the importance of datafication of church assets has been promoted. Key textbooks were written by church elders of the United Society

---

7. Cheong, "Religious Datafication."

8. Cheong, "Religious Datafication."

9. Swanson and Gardner, "The Inception and Evolution."

of Believers (or the Shakers), a religious community from 1747 to 1923, which emphasized meticulous data acquisition and the tracking of detailed records including family assets and expenditures of households living in the community.[10] In these ways, as Irvine notes, datafication with the extensive use of numbers and budgets in church records was treated as a "manifestation of holistic stewardship" to advance spiritual goals.[11]

In addition, proposals to employ specialized personnel, who may be conceived as data analysts today, have been floated in the early modern Reformed churches in Europe, as observed by Judith Pollmann.[12] A call for a quantitative examination of the records of Geneva's Reformed Consistory, the body of ministers and elders overseeing church discipline, was proposed in 1972. This call came alongside the hire of a person "able to develop statistics on the various kinds of moral aberrations . . . and establish which aberrations were most prevalent" as well as "measure how all these statistics changed over the years."[13] In other words, Christian ministry work has been conceived to entail descriptive, inferential, and longitudinal analyses of church records.

Akin to historical initiatives, many commentators have recognized the present-day enthusiasm over the notion of Big Data, with its volume, veracity, and velocity amplified by the use of mobile and digital technologies. As Jose Van Dijk points out, a dominant ideology in our networked era is "dataism," which refers to the prevalent belief in the objective quantification and monitoring of human behavior with technology, coupled with trust in institutional agents that mine and interpret data from online platforms and technologies.[14] Notably, this mind-set is also present among contemporary church leaders, who have projected positive visions and outcomes with the use of Big Data in the church.

In light of changes in the social makeup and modes of communication in US congregations, an assistant professor in religion and senior pastor of a church in Virginia, Michael Gutzler, recently argued that "for those of us who are church leaders, data collection and analysis could be the key to providing a deeper faith life to the people of congregational community."[15] Unequivocal

10. Faircloth, "The Importance of Accounting."
11. Irvine, "Balancing Money and Mission," 212.
12. Pollman, "Off the Record."
13. Pollman, "Off the Record," 423.
14. Van Dijck, "Datafication, Dataism and Dataveillance," 198.
15. Gutzler, "Big Data," 23.

support for datafication and a strong belief in dataism has been expressed, as exemplified by this affirmation, "If big data is being used to guide us in our shopping habits, could it also be used to guide people to a deeper commitment to God, faith life, and community? The answer is yes."[16] Accordingly, the main ideological equation underlying dataism may be summarized here as more data = stronger faith, as it is proposed that a "better understanding of individual and household demographics opens opportunities for a greater commitment to congregational life."[17]

A second major point, which is perhaps more muted in public discourse related to Big Data, is how datafication processes and practices are marked by church politics and power, reflecting discrimination and social inequities. Throughout history, new technological practices have also been accompanied by skepticism and moral panic over perverse outcomes. Similarly, with regard to datafication, cautionary notes have been voiced regarding elites' influence on data collection and selective reporting, resulting in error-ridden data and knowledge gaps.

For example, from a triangulation of historical documents including a diary of a Dutch church elder in the 1620s, Pollmann observed that deviant conduct of church leaders and prominent family members were often omitted from official church records and thus not catalogued.[18] These missing cases from the consistory records skewed any future data analysis. By extension, different methods of data sampling, counting, and documenting hamper meaningful cross-cultural comparisons between religious organizations, as well as over-time comparisons within the church.

Furthermore, data practices are not impersonal but embedded in religious norms. Practices of datafication are tied to changes in church governance, in response to socioeconomic conditions and technological innovations. This phenomenon was, for instance, observed in the increasing centralization of control and formalization of data-filled church reports in the episcopacy within the US capitalistic society in the 1800s, which was undergoing organizational restructuring from a state sponsored entity to an ecclesiastical enterprise.[19]

Contemporary scholarship has similarly highlighted complexities in the processes of datafication. Contrary to perceptions that digital data

16. Gutzler, "Big Data," 24.
17. Gutzler, "Big Data," 28.
18. Pollmann, "Off the Record."
19. Swanson and Gardner, "The Inception and Evolution."

collection and analysis entails merely the execution of effortless automation, assembling and transforming newly acquired data into suitable forms involve intricate and labor-intensive work. Strikingly, the first phase of most data-driven projects has been described as painstaking and laborious "data-wrangling," "data munging," and even "janitorial work."[20] Although various tools designed for specific tasks related to datafication are available, fully automated technology and software solutions accompanying the whole process are still rare. Upending the popular metaphor of "raw data," Gitelman and Jackson note that digital datasets have to be "cooked," with care and attention to political and practical decisions, even before data collection occurs.[21] Data preparation is "an iterative, multidisciplinary process," to ensure data quality, integration, reproducibility, and documentation.[22]

In sum, far from being neutral, datafication processes and practices are imbued with value judgments, politics, and bear the imprint of religious authority. The observation here about celebratory and critical views of datafication raises larger questions about its contested nature: What are the implications of dataism for the enactment of missional practice? In what ways are countervailing dynamics of datafication entwined with emerging developments and challenges to religious collectivities and governance? As new waves of data related to religious people and practices raise new opportunities and rights, it behooves us to concurrently consider risks and responsibilities for religious communities and adherents. In the next section, a discussion of a dialectical approach to religious datafication will illustrate the emergent tensions in religious identity, community, and authority.

A dialectical approach to religious datafication: tensions in missional engagement

A dialectical approach holds contradictions, known as dialectics, endemic in changes in social life. Amidst human relationships, people act and are acted upon to manage tensions.[23] This perspective provides a meta-theoretical framework for deepening understanding of digital media and religious culture as it recognizes the concurrence of two relational forces of interaction

20. Endel and Piringer, "Data Wrangling."

21. Gitelman and Jackson, "Introduction," 1–14.

22. Endel and Piringer, "Data Wrangling."

23. See Baxter and Montgomery, *Relating*, and Martin and Nakayama, "Thinking Dialectically."

and its seeming opposites.[24] Taking a dialectical approach to religious datafication prompts new considerations and questions regarding engagement, which need thoughtful reflection and communicative action to manage the complexities and frictions of contemporary religious life.

Privileged-disadvantaged religious authority and community: accelerating and altering ministry engagement

On the meso level, practices of religious datafication entwine with dialectics in the constitution of religious community and "engagement" such that religious organizations and leaders are concurrently privileged-disadvantaged. In the face of mounting datafication, religious authority is restructuring as leaders are privileged with new modes of control while also being challenged by new demands of data management, storage, and analyses. The emergence of new socialities on virtual platforms accompanied by the tracking and extraction of new flows of data and the targeting of specific audiences with tailored messages informed by big data analyses, raise new possibilities and strains in the (re)imagination of religious communities.

On the one hand, it is pertinent to recognize how church statistics and the collection of online religiously related data, including the duration and nature of online interactions, population, socio-demographics, and personal identifiable information, is being channeled by religious leadership to aid in strategic recruitment and planning, with an eye on extending growth in Christian organizations. Indeed, it has been observed that a shift in the approach to global missions has involved an uptick in attention on data-driven practices not just to demonstrate outreach effectiveness but to direct efforts of evangelistic work using particular methods with a focus on reaching specific persons of interest.[25]

From recent decades to present-day realities, a case in point is how Christian megachurches have adopted and adapted corporate marketing and entrepreneurial tech start-up strategies. A prominent aspect of their strategic operations includes the datafication of religious user behaviors to obtain insights for development and outreach efforts. In turn, data is being applied to target and connect to specific groups.

Consider how an interdenominational, evangelical church in Cincinnati, Crossroads, began its work in the mid-1980s, and appears to sustain

24. See Cheong and Ess, "Introduction," and Cheong and Arasa, "Religion."

25. Olsen, "Our April Issue."

its mission with multiple datafication practices today. A report on faith and entrepreneurship detailed how Crossroads' core founders "gathered demographic data on Cincinnatians' churchgoing habits, with a focus on the city's affluent east side. . . . They settled on a target demographic, 25–35 year old males, figuring that if they could get the guy, they would get his wife. They wrote brand positioning statements . . . Finally, they built a slide deck featuring a mix of data and Scripture and began raising money from friends, family and business connections."[26] This megachurch has been recognized as the fourth largest and fastest growing church in America,[27] operates in thirteen locations, and has a staff of 300 members (Crossroads.net), including a large "experience team" that fields church data collection through "in-church clicker surveys" and leverages data from their app. The church also has an "IT mission" with the stated goal of "accelerating ministry through technology, data, training, and process improvements."

Besides the above example that highlights various ways in which data is captured and applied in a North American church setting, there are churches worldwide that have created or customized church and mobile app technologies, tools that are designed to jointly connect followers and track religious interactions. In conjunction with the promotion of church apps for facilitating regular and repeated interactions with religious leadership, pastoral team members in Asia have utilized digital apps to advance church-led social media campaigns.[28] Correspondingly, it is not uncommon to find popular church mobile applications being promoted as driving community growth and outreach, and even labelled as "The *Ultimate Engagement* Platform" (https://www.subsplash.com/), "the *best way to engage* your congregation anytime, anywhere" (sharefaith.com) and "church management" tools to "*Super-Charge Engagement*" (churchbase.com) with "seamless integration" between platforms, and multiple church analytics for downloads (italics for emphasis, mine). Here, it is also particularly interesting to note how we are witnessing the entry of socially networked, app-enabled data analytics into the waters of faith, where intensifying efforts are applied to push new "data frontiers"[29] into local and global missional work.

Besides apps that provide a digital church presence and track user data, there are additional services and tools available for the calculation

---

26. Frazier, "What Would Jesus Disrupt?"

27. *Outreach Magazine.*

28. See Cheong, "Religious datafication," and Cheong, "Tweet the Message?"

29. Beer, "Envisioning the Power."

and visualization of church data, that are framed as being directly tied to church growth. For example, churchmetrics.com (taglined as "see trends and make better decisions to grow your church") provides churches with an account to help them input and track their data, including patterns of their volunteer involvement, giving, attendance, baptisms, and even cars in the parking lot. Data is collated and represented into customizable charts and dashboards. The site also showcases possibilities for data cor-relation with other datasets as their "weather integration feature" provides a way in which weather information can be integrated into church infor-mation like adult attendance figures.

Hence, as growth in religious community and church engagement are (re)presented as inextricably linked to app use and its attendant datafica-tion, religious authority now involves the duty to understand how signifi-cant concepts like church attendance and salvation are being transformed into data points and reports. In this way, dialectics in the restructuring of religious authority and community appear to correlate with emergences of datafication processes and practices operant in churches today. On the one hand, religious leaders are now privileged with new modes of "knowing" and control. Empowered with new databases, they can glean insights from more data, see patterns by matching datasets, and perform longitudinal analyses of their congregants' interactions, which may in turn inform or drive their decision making and outreach efforts to grow the church.

At the same time, religious leaders may concurrently experience new stresses as they are faced with new forms of time and labor pressures ex-pended on data collection and input, together with emerging needs to man-age new technical systems of data analyses and storage. Data deluge and overload can dim decision making, and ironically lead to less efficient opera-tions.[30] The datafication of religious user behavior also becomes problematic when missional concerns or behaviors are inferred from limited quantita-tive measures. For example, in widely used promotional discourse of church apps, manifest variables of church growth and "engagement" (i.e. observable behaviors, like headcount comparisons or online clicks) are associated with latent (i.e. unobservable) missional goals, like community growth. Data-led processes to measure growth with a limited time span of analysis might also be imperfectly equated with the community reflected in the New Testament Greek conception of koinonia that is profoundly cultivated in mutuality, partnership, and accountability over time.

30. Tenner, *The Efficiency Paradox.*

Prior social scientific research on quantifying educational outcomes show that quantitative indicators applied toward decision making is subject to corruption of the social processes it intended to monitor[31] and apparent well-intentioned church planting solutions may have unintended consequences which can worsen problems in the long term (i.e. the cobra effect, referenced for example in Brickman, *Preparing the 21st Century Church*). Subsequently, it is possible to reach quantitative engagement indicators (i.e. attendance, "like" or "click" targets) through means that distort and undermine the real desired outcome (biblical fellowship). Religious organizations and leaders may also be stuck in a locked-in scenario as datafication is related to the escalator effect or irreversible act of ascending commitment and costs. In an earlier but related setting of intense technological adoption, research has shown that individuals who have invested in networking technologies for critical tasks are often committed to these new capacities and potentials, whether they eventually find them fruitful or not.[32]

In addition, it is worth highlighting that datafication via the use of church metrics have variable outcomes for different clergy in different contexts, depending on their size (and the attendant statistical power for inferential analysis based on the scope of their data collection). As Karl Vaters explains, "[I]n healthy small churches, average numbers will not be typical numbers" since "some small churches are small enough that they don't need additional small groups (how would you do small groups in a church of 12, for instance?), while other small churches might have a couple of small groups with every member of the congregation active in one." Therefore, it has been recommended that we recognize how "small churches are a unique part of the body of Christ" and that some churches need to "assess health and effectiveness in more qualitative ways than quantitative."[33] In short, while balancing the excitement over Big Data and church metrics, religious leaders and organizations must remain attentive to ministry context, commitment, and motivation, to "why people do things, write things, or make things . . . in the sheer volume of numbers," not least for the reason that "bigger data are not always better data."[34]

---

31. Campbell, "Assessing the Impact."

32. Rochlin, *Trapped in the Net*.

33. Vaters, "Effective Small Church."

34. Boyd and Crawford, "Critical Questions," 66–67.

Privileged-disadvantaged religious identity and participation: asymmetric platforms and digital literacies for personal engagement

As datafication processes undergird and mediate social and online interactions, notions of self and identity, which are composed of our basic understandings and assumptions of how such selves may and/or must share data in order to relate to larger groups are changing. Religious followers are privileged-disadvantaged as they engage and are engaged by digital media and its accompanying forms of datafication.

On the one hand, personal religious piety can be nurtured through multiple mediated modes since online sacred and linked texts, commentaries, and devotionals serve many as convenient resources, and networked audio-visual data streams help fulfill immediate needs and inquiries (e.g. various "Church TV" channels, and "RightNow" online streaming videos). Religious users are now empowered with new choices and access to curated platforms for their edification and education, while Big Data is being harvested from the routine and quotidian ways in which faith practitioners use online media to read and share. As mediated religious platforms are becoming more globally accessible, religious geocoded Big Data can be collected internationally, to illuminate regional- or national-level comparisons, which can in turn be used to tailor content and enhance user experiences.

A case in point here is how the mobile Bible app, YouVersion, with over 350 million installs in unique devices worldwide, has drawn from user interactions or what it has termed "Bible engagement" online, to shape its platform and report a range of user statistics (https://share.bible.com/2018/). These statistics include user location, the most popular Bible verses shared, bookmarked, and highlighted, chapters read, audio chapters played, emojis tapped, and ratings of Bible reading plans.

On an individual level, the recording of user activity statistics online may serve as visual reminders to motivate users toward greater interaction and achieve their Bible reading goals. In line with their blog tagline to "engage Scripture like never before," the app also employs game design elements and incentives like the awarding of badges to those recognized as accomplished Bible readers.[35]

Yet while some religious individuals are prompted to log their Bible reading and share their notes or favorite verses, religious identities are

35. Hutchings, "Now the Bible."

simultaneously being shaped as they are cultivated toward distinctive forms of habitual interaction for platform user retention.[36] In the case of YouVersion, Timothy Hutchings observed that users access this online Christian application "through an interface designed to visually and procedurally emphasize sharing. . . . [W]hen we look at the actual choice of texts to share . . . very specific categories of Bible text flourish while others attract less attention."[37]

Indeed, the configuration of this Bible reading application has been purportedly shaped by insights from Big Data. After an examination of the app and interview with its founder, Nir Eyal concluded that the app's infrastructure and content are constantly being monitored, updated, and fine-tuned, by "marrying the principles of consumer psychology with the latest in big data analytics."[38] Using user behavioral data as feedback enabled a reconfiguration of the app to facilitate changes in how users interact with specific religious texts, as relayed by the founder who said "his data also revealed that changing the order of the Bible, placing the more interesting sections up-front and saving the boring bits for later increased Bible reading plan completion rates."[39]

In this sense, the emergence of a pious self vis-à-vis online "Bible engagement" facilitated by datafication is at once a privilege and a product of algorithmic relations. Tensions may ensue when particular selves do not respond to features (notifications, reminders, "daily streaks," and "Perfect Weeks"), or fail to perform to planned goals, and are thus not recognized or rewarded, according to optimal standards of "engagement" as recorded and marked by the app. Hence, to a certain extent, dataveillance or the systematic monitoring of people or groups by means of personal data systems in order to regulate or govern their behavior,[40] is enacted here.

The (re)assembling of the app interface derived from Big Data insights to promote certain forms of online interactions also has implications for how religious individuals comment and share, and thereby how their identities may be shifting to more relational selves facilitated through the construction of particular account histories, "Bible App Friends," and social feed triggers.

36. Cheong, "Religious Datafication."

37. Hutchings, "Now the Bible," 25.

38. Eyal, *Hooked.*

39. Eyal, *Hooked,* 187.

40. Van Dijck, "Datafication, Dataism and Dataveillance."

This vision of the power of data engineering to manage religious users' behaviors is observed, for instance, in YouVersion's tenth anniversary press release, which reported that "beyond shaping the way we interact with Scripture and each other, the Bible App has introduced a way for the Bible to reach us in our everyday lives . . ."[41] Each new feature is targeted to increase daily engagement from the YouVersion community, since by adding features like daily Streaks and Perfect Weeks, the number of daily active users has increased by more than 30 percent compared to last year."[42] In short, religious users are distinctively positioned and targeted for particular modes of engagement as data is not only collected and archived from routine reading and sharing, but datafication is also applied to change the conditions and environment in which religious individuals act and connect to each other and to sacred texts.

Furthermore, the notion of "Bible engagement" may be constrained by multiple structural- and individual-level digital divides. As Internet access becomes more readily available worldwide, and as "user friendly" digital applications and "smart technologies" abound, digital inequalities are changing. Contrary to earlier predictions of the demise of digital access gaps, material access to costly digital gadgets appear to be resurfacing as a primary divide in terms of the prices of devices escalating with every upgrade that is bundled with new features and increased computing power.

Beyond primary-level access divides, new digital literacies are needed to interact online as religious adherents and seekers navigate and manage faith-based mediated content and networks. Of particular relevance to datafication are a) the skills to present an authentic self, amidst a culture of personal branding and religious celebrification,[43] and b) the ability to mitigate privacy and security risks within the increasingly interconnected ecosystem of the Internet of things.[44]

As we have noted, "a paradox of religious identity in our networked age concern how one's religious identity represented through communication technologies becomes simultaneously more authentic and accessible, as well as more edited and polished than in face to face settings."[45] This tension may be deepened as contemporary practices of datafication

---

41. YouVersion, "Bible App Celebrates."

42. YouVersion, "Bible App Celebrates."

43. Cheong, "Religious Authority."

44. Kshetri, "Big Data."

45. Cheong and Arasa, "Religion."

amplify social distance and exacerbate inequalities between online in-fluencers who are able to use data to boost their platform visibility, and those who cannot or do not.

Closely related to the above is another key divide emerging with big data analytics: between those who have the capacities to extract, collect, process (and profit from) data, and those whom data collection targets.[46] Here, it is significant to note how contemporary datafication and its risks to individuals are linked to how Christian leaders and entities are collecting data in present-day ecosystems of connected apps, devices, and sensors. Some churches either do not readily provide information on their data privacy policy or use jargon-filled templates online that may not be easily understood by their congregants.

It is also questionable when Christian organizations pressure or mandate the use of certain digital applications or devices, which are ostensibly encouraged to provide certain features use, while these same applications act as data monitoring tools with a reach that may not be fully acknowledged or recognized by users, and linked to undesirable outcomes. For example, related concerns here were raised when Oral Roberts University, a four-year liberal arts Christian college in Tulsa, Oklahoma, began to require all freshmen and transfer students to wear a Fitbit (digital wearable and fitness tracker) as part of an introductory physical fitness course. To earn 20 percent of their course grade, students have to walk at least 10,000 steps daily and record 150 minutes of physical activity as measured by heart rate, with this activity tracking information being made available to their professor.

While the use of biometric data to manage religious bodies in Christian institutions is not new,[47] and university officials have praised its convenience, efficacy, and benefits to students,[48] critics have pointed out various limitations and advantages for individuals that appear to be muted in official discourse. Besides the added cost of purchasing a fitness band, it is debatable if data produced by Fitbit is accurate, or will lead to better health outcomes,[49] particularly for those who struggle with obses-sive exercise and eating disorders.[50] Activity rates can also be rigged by

46. Andrejevic, "Big Data."

47. Root, "How Fitbit Helps."

48. Sherman, "Fitbit Monitoring Program."

49. Landsbaum, "Why a Christian University's."

50. McNeal, "People Are Furious."

users. There are further questions on how Fitbit, a commercial company, will protect user data on their accounts, or handle potential data hacks or a data breach on their cloud software. While students retain the right to scrub their data from the Fitbit account upon graduation, and the data is not purportedly linked to location tracking, the issue of individual engagement remains a vexed one.

Concerns voiced over personal data collection in other related contexts have highlighted different and multiple dimensions of a Big Data divide.[51] These dimensions include users' miscomprehension of their informed consent and terms of use, and an expressed sense of powerlessness and lack of knowledge about the possible use of personal information and anticipated harms, that are not yet fully understood by any entity ("what individuals can do with their data in isolation differs strikingly from what various data collectors can do with this same data in the broader context of everyone else's data").[52] For some, there may also be a perceived loss of control, lack of options, and opportunity costs of nonparticipation. It has been reported that no ORU student has since opted for the prior pen-and-paper means of activity tracking,[53] but it is worth noting in this case that no other digitized method for logging activity data has been offered.

As a related aside, my ongoing interdisciplinary and mixed methods research on IoT, digital skills, and privacy among college students, tied to participation in my university's seven-college IoT innovation collective, has recently examined a case where a voice-based digital assistant was freely provided to all engineering students in a residence hall (students had to sign a lengthy waiver for device use), but this practice has since been changed given some students' negative feedback and expressed concerns about their privacy.[54] Thus, when individuals are compelled to share their data via technical systems that are increasingly sophisticated with data collection and mining, a distaste for policy (or lack thereof) may erode institutional trust and public attitudes toward power asymmetries (in both the above cases, involving partnerships of educational institutions and technology firms) in datafication practices.

---

51. Andrejevic, "Big Data."
52. Andrejevic, "Big Data," 1674.
53. Sherman, "Fitbit Monitoring Program."
54. Thomason, "ASU Tooker House."

Conclusion: toward data discernment

In a networked era of digital applications, social media, and connected devices, to understand missional engagement is to understand how religious related data is being imagined and treated, and the types of digital applications that are being deployed. In addition to this, this chapter suggests, it is important to explore the dialectics of datafication and ways in which they intersect with emerging tensions in the constitution of religious authority, community, and identity. Beyond extreme visions of technological optimism and pessimism, understanding how religious collectives and individual lives are privileged and disadvantaged in light of datafication illuminates new concerns about missional work and raises questions for future reflections.

Specifically, within the discourse of present-day IoT and the potential for people to connect to their social networks through any *smart* device, the notion of my *digital neighbor* is likely to be more varied and complex. This is not least because a growing number of religious actors (human and nonhuman algorithms, etc.) are both creating as well as responding to data visions and flows. As the availability of new social media and digital applications have grown, exposure to immediate and suggested "friends" are widened as platforms prompt structured, even regular data sharing. In turn, growing digital "engagement" in a networked era, has taken on greater significance, as discussed in prior examples related to church digital apps and the promotion of app-enabled Bible reading experiences.

Furthermore, as explicated in this article, within an IoT infrastructure, an assemblage of religious software, platforms, and databases forms a central hub of how data about one's religious interactions are mined, (re) presented, interpreted, and then incorporated into organizational structures and decision making. As this might suggest, spiritual leaders and adherents are privileged-disadvantaged as they utilize new resources and features of connectivity, while being at the same time faced with new costs of participation and inequalities that are not easily overcome.

More attention in the future might be paid to how clergy and laity cope and manage these dialectics, with added consideration of how datafied operations shape our concept of ourselves and our neighbors. As Nick Couldry and Jannis Kallinikos caution, "On social media, users for practical purposes are not real persons but abstract operations enacted through the aggregation of singular data-points."[55] It is thus significant with Big Data operations that we honor explanation and meaning, alongside our quest for prediction and correlation so as not to undermine the empowering potential of digital and social media. At present, a focus on the creation of value from digital platforms appears to justify swift roll-outs of new applications and/or new pressures to be early adopters and innovators with new media. These pressures can affect leaders and laity in church settings and beyond. Yet the dialectics of datafication highlight how new data can simultaneously unite and divide us, facilitating the fostering of new ties while fracturing other social contracts.

Loving our neighbor as ourselves entails but is not limited to, an attention to these underappreciated tensions in context, including circumspection of the rights and privacy of individual persons in their everyday and quotidian affairs online. As C. S. Lewis pointedly put it, "There are no ordinary people . . . Next to the Blessed sacrament itself, your neighbor is the holiest object presented to your senses."[56] Insofar as digital technologies are evolving quickly and becoming (in)visibly embedded in our routine rhythms and networks with relatively little public scrutiny and ambivalence, an interdisciplinary outlook undertaken by collaboratives like Fuller Theological Seminary's missiology lecture series, helps advance our duty of data discernment in a networked era.

Bibliography

Anderson, Janna Quitney, and Harrison Rainie. *The Future of Big Data*. Washington, DC: Pew Internet & American Life Project, 2012.

Andrejevic, Mark. "Big Data, Big Questions: The Big Data Divide." *International Journal of Communication* 8 (2014) 1673–89.

Baxter, Leslie A., and Barbara M. Montgomery. *Relating: Dialogues and Dialectics*. New York: Guilford, 1996.

Beer, David. "Envisioning the Power of Data Analytics." *Information, Communication & Society* 21.3 (2018) 465–79.

Boyd, Danah, and Kate Crawford. "Critical Questions for Big Data: Provocations for a Cultural, Technological, and Scholarly Phenomenon." *Information, Communication & Society* 15.5 (2012) 662–79.

Brickman, Leslie H. *Preparing the 21st Century Church*. N.p.: Xulon, 2002.

Campbell, Donald T. "Assessing the Impact of Planned Social Change." *Evaluation and Program Planning* 2.1 (1979) 67–90.

---

55. Couldry and Kallinikos, "Ontology," 153.

56. Lewis, *The Weight of Glory*, 46.

Chen, Min, Shiwen Mao, and Yunhao Liu. "Big Data: A Survey." *Mobile Networks and Applications* 19.2 (2014) 171–209.

Cheong, Pauline. "Religious Datafication: Platforms, Practices and Power." In *The Routledge Handbook of Religion and Journalism,* edited by K. Radde-Antweiler and X. Zeiler. London: Routledge, forthcoming.

———. "Church Digital Applications and the Communicative Meso-Micro Interplay: Building Religious Authority and Community Through Everyday Organizing." In *Mediatized Religion in Asia,* 105–18. London: Routledge, 2018.

———. "Religious Authority and Social Media Branding in a Culture of Religious Celebrification." In *The Media and Religious Authority,* edited by Stuart M. Hoover, 81–104. University Park, PA: The Pennsylvania State University Press, 2016.

———. "Tweet the Message? Religious Authority and Social Media Innovation." *Journal of Religion, Media and Digital Culture* 3.3 (2014) 1–19.

———, and Daniel Arasa. "Religion." In *Handbooks of Communication Science, Vol 5. Communication and Technology,* edited by L. Cantoni and J. Danowski, 455–66. Berlin: De Gruyter Mouton, 2015.

———, and Charles Ess. "Introduction: Religion 2.0? Relational and Hybridizing Pathways in Religion, Social Media, and Culture." In *Digital Religion, Social Media and Culture,* 1–21. New York: Peter Lang, 2012.

Couldry, Nick, and Jannis Kallinikos. "Ontology." In *The SAGE Handbook of Social Media,* edited by Jean Burgess, Alice Marwick, and Thomas Poell, 146–59. London: Sage, 2017.

Cukier, Kenneth, and Viktor Mayer-Schoenberger. "The Rise of Big Data: How It's Changing the Way We Think about the World." *Foreign Affairs* 92 (2013) 28–40.

Endel, Florian, and Harald Piringer. "Data Wrangling: Making data useful again." *IFAC-PapersOnLine* 48.1 (2015) 111–12.

Eyal, N. *Hooked: How to Build Habit-Forming Products.* New York: Penguin, 2014.

Faircloth, Archie. "The Importance of Accounting to the Shakers." *Accounting Historians Journal* 15.2 (1988) 99–129.

Frazier, Mya. "What Would Jesus Disrupt?" *Bloomberg,* April 5, 2017. https://www.bloomberg.com/news/features/2017-04-05/what-would-jesus-disrupt.

Gitelman, Lisa, and V. Jackson. "Introduction." In *"Raw Data" Is an Oxymoron,* edited by L. Gitelman, 1–14. Cambridge, MA: MIT Press, 2013.

Gutzler, Michael D. "Big Data and the 21st Century Church." *Dialog* 53.1 (2014) 23–29.

Harari, Yuval Noah. *Homo Deus: A Brief History of Tomorrow.* New York: Random House, 2016.

Hutchings, Tim. "Now the Bible Is an App: Digital Media and Changing Patterns of Religious Authority." In *Religion, Media, and Social Change,* edited by K. Granholm, M. Moberg, and S. Sjo, 151–69. London: Routledge, 2014.

Irvine, Helen. "Balancing Money and Mission in a Local Church Budget." *Accounting, Auditing & Accountability Journal* 18.2 (2005) 211–37.

Kshetri, Nir. "Big Data's Impact on Privacy, Security and Consumer Welfare." *Telecommunications Policy* 38.11 (2014) 1134–45.

Landsbaum, Claire. "Why a Christian's University Freshman Fitbit Requirement Is a Bad Idea." February 4, 2016. https://www.thecut.com/2016/02/christian-school-requires-fitbits-for-freshmen.html.

Lewis, C. S. *The Weight of Glory.* San Francisco: HarperOne, 2015.

Martin, Judith N., and Thomas K. Nakayama. "Thinking Dialectically about Culture and Communication." *Communication Theory* 9.1 (1999) 1–25.

McNeal, Stephanie. "People Are Furious with this College for Making Its Freshmen Wear Fitbits." *Buzzfeed,* April 17, 2016 https://www.buzzfeednews.com/article/stephaniemcneal/fitbit-requirement.

Olsen, Andy. "Our April Issue: Strength in Numbers." *Christianity Today,* March 15, 2019. https://www.christianitytoday.com/ct/2019/april/our-april-issue-strength-in-numbers.html.

Pollmann, Judith. "Off the Record: Problems in the Quantification of Calvinist Church Discipline." *The Sixteenth Century Journal* 33.2 (Summer 2002) 423–38.

Reinsel, D., J. Gantz, and J. Rydning. "Data Age 2025: The Evolution of Data to Life-Critical." International Data Corporation, 2017. https://www.seagate.com/www-content/our-story/trends/files/Seagate-WP-DataAge2025-March-2017.pdf.

Rochlin, Gene I. *Trapped in the Net: The Unanticipated Consequences of Computerization.* Princeton, NJ: Princeton University Press, 1997.

Root, Jonathan. "How Fitbit Helps a Conservative Evangelical College Monitor Students' Bodies for Christ." *Religion Dispatches,* March 10, 2016. http://religiondispatches.org/where-oral-meets-orwell/.

Sherman, Bill. "Fitbit Monitoring Program a Hit at ORU." *Tulsa World,* March 20, 2017. https://www.tulsaworld.com/news/local/fitbit-fitness-monitoring-program-a-hit-at-oru/article_eae41a5e-830a-5270-98de-c1aa62aac28d.html.

Swanson, G. A., and John C. Gardner. "The Inception and Evolution of Financial Reporting in the Protestant Episcopal Church in the United States of America." *Accounting Historians Journal* 13.2 (1986) 55–63.

Tenner, Edward. *The Efficiency Paradox: What Big Data Can't Do.* New York: Vintage, 2018.

Thomason, Ashlee. "ASU Tooker House Residents Disappointed with Donated Amazon Echo Dots." November 7, 2017. https://mylocalnews.us/arizona/2017/11/asu-tooker-house-residents-disappointed-with-donated-amazon-echo-dots/.

Van Dijck, José. "Datafication, Dataism and Dataveillance: Big Data Between Scientific Paradigm and Ideology." *Surveillance & Society* 12.2 (2014) 197–208.

Vaters, Karl. "Effective Small Church Metrics: Why Average Results Aren't Typical Results." *Christianity Today,* February 8, 2019. https://www.christianitytoday.com/karl-vaters/2019/february/small-church-metrics-average-typical-results.html.

YouVersion. "Bible App Celebrates 10th Anniversary." https://www.youversion.com/press/youversion-bible-app-celebrates-10th-anniversary/.

Part III

How does one become a (digital) neighbor?

CHAPTER 5

Positive Youth Development & Technology

*Developing Character in Youth in the
Present Technological Landscape*[1]

S ARAH S CHNITKER ,

K UTTER C ALLAWAY ,

A ND M ADISON K AWAKAMI G ILBERTSON

A ny observer of adolescent social behavior in recent years will quickly
notice that most teen interactions include a smartphone—whether adolescents are physically present with each other or apart. Research overwhelmingly supports the premise that technologically mediated social contexts are ubiquitous for adolescents and young adults today. As of 2018, 95 percent of teens (thirteen- to seventeen-year-olds) living in the US have access to

1. We would like to thank Matt Lumpkin from Tidepool and Matthew Geddert from Curly Robot for their collaborative efforts in creating the CharacterMe app. We would also like to thank Dr. Benjamin Houltberg at University of Southern California, Dr. Jennifer Shubert at Baylor University, Dr. Lixian Cui at New York University Shanghai, and Dr. Kenneth Wang at Fuller Seminary for their contributions to the design, implementation, and analyses of the study. The preparation of this chapter was supported by a grant from the John Templeton Foundation. The opinions expressed in this publication are those of the authors and do not necessarily reflect the views of the John Templeton Foundation. Correspondence concerning this chapter should be addressed to Dr. Sarah A. Schnitker, Psychology and Neuroscience, One Bear Place 97334, Baylor University, Waco, TX 76798-7334. Email: Sarah_Schnitker@baylor.edu.

a smartphone and 45 percent say they are online "almost constantly."[2] Moreover, this reported access to smartphones is unrelated to income such that adolescents across the economic spectrum have equal access. A study by Common Sense Media found that adolescents in the United States use an average of nine hours of media daily (not including for school/homework).[3] Adolescent males in the US spend an average of fifty-six minutes a day playing video games, and teen girls spend an average of one hour and thirty-two minutes on social media.[4] These trends extend to other cultures as well. In South Korea, 95.9 percent of teenagers reported using a smartphone, and even in twenty-one developing countries, a median of 54 percent of the general populations use the Internet occasionally or own a smartphone.[5]

Many adults who did not grow up in the age of information find these trends alarming and fear youth are doomed. There may be some good cause for this fear. Research on smartphone and social media use suggests that, at least in some ways, technology has made it more difficult for adolescents to "love their neighbor." Numerous studies have found negative effects of technology and media use in adolescents. For example, mobile devices have been linked to decreases in emotional intelligence and empathic abilities, and video games have long been criticized as increasing aggression.[6] Even social media usage has been deemed problematic as research finds it may breed envy, anxiety, and narcissism.[7] Some scholars have speculated that the asynchronous time delay of social media communication may erode social competencies (e.g., Turkle).[8] Likewise, Jean Twenge's analysis of historical trends suggests that this hyper-connected generation of young people are displaying unprecedented levels of loneliness, anxiety, and depression.[9]

And yet these technologies are not going away, nor are their potential benefits necessarily outweighed by these troubling trends. Might these technological tools be redeemed to promote human flourishing? No doubt,

2. Anderson and Jiang, "Teens, Social Media & Technology 2018."

3. Common Sense Media, "The Common Sense Census."

4. Common Sense Media, "The Common Sense Census."

5. Korea Internet and Security Agency, *2016 Survey on Internet Usage*.

6. Misra et al., "The iPhone Effect"; Przybylski and Weinstein, "Can You Connect with Me Now?"; Anderson and Bushman, "Effects of Violent Video Games."

7. Krasnova et al., "Envy on Facebook"; Rosen et al., "Is Facebook Creating 'iDisorders'?"; Buffardi and Campbell, "Narcissism and Social Networking."

8. Turkle, *Alone Together*.

9. Twenge, *iGen*.

technological advances are powerful forces in society, but members of these technologically advanced societies can find productive ways to counter negative trends and use technology for virtue development. In particular, new technologies yield unprecedented levels of engagement and access to young people that can be harnessed to promote positive spiritual and virtue formation. Rather than trying to persuade adolescents to turn off their devices (a nearly impossible task) to engage in character development activities, adults should capitalize on the access to the inner lives of teens by locating character strength interventions where youth are already spending their time—on their screens. Several attempts have been made to cultivate virtues and character in adolescents through new technologies in recent years. However, these preliminary attempts need further development and a stronger evidence base supporting their efficacy.

As it concerns Christian mission, some resistance to this kind of technological development and innovation is to be expected. In Janet H. Murray's historical analysis and uncannily accurate predictions for the twenty-first century, she argues nearly all major technological innovations—from the novel to computers—have been criticized for their ability to "reshape the spectrum of narrative expression," which widens or expands the human experience.[10] Such expansion is often met with fear and suspicion. Rather than simply give in to these fears, missiologists and theologians may choose, instead, to recognize the missiological significance of new technologies by constructing a more robust theological understanding of technology's many possibilities.

How Might New Technology Promote Virtue and Spiritual Development?

There are a variety of ways digital technology might enhance the religious and spiritual lives of young people, but a focus on using technology to cultivate virtues is one of the most promising. Virtue formation approaches to spiritual growth have experienced a slowly growing resurgence of popularity in the past decade (likely spurred by the clarity of N. T. Wright's defense in *After You Believe*).[11] In addition, recent developmental and personality psychology theories on virtue development in adolescents

---

10. Murray, *Hamlet on the Holodeck*.
11. Wright, *After You Believe*.

maintain that virtues comprise adaptive habits connected to a transcendent or moral narrative identity.[12]

Whereas many religious communities tend to focus on the overarching narrative of their particular tradition and (in healthy contexts) how that narrative can be integrated with a young person's own identity to build virtue, fewer religious groups have effective means of helping adolescents to form new habits or replace old habits, both of which are necessary for virtue development. This is likely because changing habits is quite difficult and requires practice across many days or months; research shows it takes between eighteen and 254 days to form a simple habit (e.g., "eating a piece of fruit with lunch," "running 15 minutes before dinner").[13] Additionally, many of the traditional liturgical practices that might support habit formation for virtues (e.g., fasting) have been largely abandoned by evangelicals, who have tended to underestimate the effects of liturgical practice on formation.[14] Thus, technological tools may fill a gap in religious contexts and in society more broadly.

Habit Formation

Habit formation requires both individualized and contextualized practice whereby actions (even those that are complex) become automatically activated when people encounter particular situations or environments.[15] Given that situations involving other people are highly salient for virtue development (e.g., it is hard to practice love if you are not interacting with another person), habit formation around virtue, in particular, necessitates social integration. Given these necessary conditions for the formation of habits that build virtue, technology may be uniquely suited to create such situations.

Psychologists Stephen Schueller, Ricardo Muñoz, and David Mohr recognize three key affordances of digital technologies for changing habits and behavior: personalization, connecting people, and mass dissemination of information.[16] The personalization provided by smartphone tech-

12. Schnitker et al., "Religion, Spirituality, and Thriving."

13. Carden and Wood, "Habit Formation and Change"; Lally et al., "How Are Habits Formed."

14. See, for example, the recent work in this area by James K. A. Smith, *You Are What You Love.*

15. Carden and Wood, "Habit Formation and Change."

16. Schueller et al., "Realizing the Potential."

nology, in particular, allows for a virtue intervention to be contextualized and integrated in the daily lives of young people, such that teens are connected to those situations that can trigger habits. Likewise, the ability of smartphones to connect people—and their prominence in adolescent interpersonal relationships—also makes smartphones a ripe location for virtue development.

Challenges and Solutions

However, creating technology that cultivates these virtues is no easy task. It is challenging to fashion technology that provides a positive user experience whereby teens voluntarily engage a product because the psychological mechanisms that will build virtue may oppose the mechanisms that typically make products popular. In fact, it might be argued that many apps are popular with teens *precisely because* they tap into the very psychological processes that underlie many of the vices. For example, the gamification and reinforcement schedules provided in many apps (e.g., Angry Birds, Candy Crush) may foster addictive behaviors and undermine intrinsic motivation for engaging in leisure activities, especially in certain types of users.[17] Although social media apps (e.g., Instagram, Snapchat) may help teens to make social connections, these apps may also (a) increase excessive self focus, (b) activate social comparison processes that increase unhealthy pride and undermine humility, and (c) promote gossip and relational aggression given the deindividuation that can occur without the physical presence of others.[18] Teens, themselves, recognize the promises and pitfalls of social media. A recent survey by Pew Research Center revealed that 31 percent of US teens say social media has a mostly positive effect on people their own age (primarily because it helps them connect with family and friends), but 24 percent of teens say social media has a mostly negative effect on people their age (primarily because it prevents in-person contact/relationship building and promotes bullying, rumor spreading, unrealistic views of others' lives, and addiction/distraction).[19]

Given the potential pitfalls and obstacles for building smartphone apps or other products that cultivate virtue, an interdisciplinary approach is necessary to ensure that new products are both attractive to teens and

17. Van Deursen et al., "Modeling Habitual and Addictive."
18. Nesi and Prinstein, "Using Social."
19. Anderson and Jiang, "Teens, Social Media & Technology 2018."

actually build virtue (and do not build vice!). Technology designers and developers need to partner with scientists who have expertise in the psychological underpinnings of adolescent and virtue development as well as the training to test the efficacy of products. Moreover, practical theologians and missiologists are needed in this work to articulate the spiritual significance of what is taking place as well as help young people connect their technology use to their representation of faith in their narrative identities. Such cross-disciplinary collaboration is difficult, but the payoff is well worth the extra effort.

Building the Virtue of Patience with a Smartphone App

Patience is a core Christian virtue and arguably one of the most eroded by technological developments. Even before the information revolution of the late 1990s, theologian and moral philosopher David Bailey Harned was arguing that patience had, in fact, been declining in Western Christendom—in both its importance and practice—since the technological innovations of the Industrial Revolution.[20] He suggested that, because technologies provide vast reductions in many forms of physical suffering, patience is increasingly perceived as "outdated." Thus, waiting and suffering are seen as a "deprivation enforced upon us by an unfriendly environment," and patience has "frequently seemed childlike . . . [,] an unimaginative failure of nerve."[21] However, Harned also pointed out that "affluence and inventiveness have not so much reduced our time waiting as simply changed it."[22] Indeed, Timex estimates that across a lifetime, people spend six months waiting in lines, forty-three days on hold with automated customer service lines, and twenty-seven days waiting for the bus (for those who use public transport).[23] Moreover, psychological forms of suffering that require patience to bear well (e.g., mental illness) have, if anything, increased in recent years among adolescents.[24]

---

20. Harned, *Patience*.

21. Harned, *Patience*, 3.

22. Harned, *Patience*, 3.

23. Logistics at MGEPS at UPV, "How Much Time of an Average Life Is Spent Waiting?"; Business Wire, "Where Does the Time Go?"

24. Twenge, *iGen*.

The Psychology of Patience

Psychologists who study patience define it as the ability to be calm in the face of frustration, adversity, or suffering.[25] Although Westerners may associate patience with passivity, weakness, or inaction, scientific studies demonstrate that patience is uncorrelated with assertiveness and actually facilitates effortful goal pursuit.[26] These findings are consistent with classical virtue theory, which maintains virtues are the golden mean between two poles of vice, representing excess and deficiency.[27] Patience can be construed as the mean between recklessness and sloth/disengagement. Moreover, patience is related to a host of positive outcomes (e.g., higher life satisfaction, positive emotions, regulated behavior) as well as higher religiousness and spirituality in adolescents.[28] Even among groups of people who experience intense suffering—such as those hospitalized for inpatient psychiatric treatment—patience may serve as a resource for healing.[29] Most compellingly (from a scientific perspective), adults randomly assigned to engage in patience-building activities demonstrate the ability to grow in patience as well as exhibit subsequent gains in communicative competence, social support, positive emotions, and mental health compared to people assigned to a control group.[30]

Research on patience reveals three potential "types" or varieties of patience: interpersonal patience, life-hardship patience, and daily hassles patience.[31] The Latin root for patience is *pati*, which means "to suffer."[32] These three types of patience relate to how well people are able to endure various sources of suffering. Although people often think of daily hassles—waiting in lines, getting stuck in traffic—when they first think about patience, this type of patience is less foundational for a thriving moral life characterized by prosocial engagement. Instead, life-hardship patience (e.g., being able to wait out tough times, like a life illness) and interpersonal patience (e.g.,

25. Schnitker, "An Examination of Patience and Well-Being."

26. Schnitker, "An Examination of Patience and Well-Being."

27. Rorty, *Essays on Aristotle's Ethics.*

28. Schnitker et al., "Longitudinal Study of Religious and Spiritual Transformation"; Schnitker et al., "Efficacy of Self-Control"; Schnitker et al., "The Virtue of Patience."

29. Schnitker et al., "Patient Patients."

30. Lavelock et al., "Good Things Come"; Schnitker et al., "Religion, Spirituality, and Thriving."

31. Schnitker, "An Examination of Patience and Well-Being."

32. Oxford University Press, "Patience."

remaining calm when other people are frustrating) are more typically associated with other moral virtues and positive interpersonal outcomes.[33] Interpersonal patience, in particular, is essential for prosocial action and healthy relationships, and it is likely of greatest interest to many Christians who seek to follow Christ's greatest commands to love God and love our neighbors (Mark 12:30–31). In other words, patience is key to the Christian's ability to participate in the God's ongoing mission in the world.

When thinking about how the virtue of patience develops in young people, psychologists describe the primary habits undergirding patience as centered around more effectively regulating emotions in response to frustrations. Likewise, they hypothesize that patience is cultivated when adolescents' narrative identities allow them to make transcendent, or beyond-the-self, meaning of suffering.[34] Thus, adolescents need opportunities to build new habits around regulating emotions in their daily lives and construct (or reconstruct) their narrative identity to include transcendent meaning to increase patience. Religious communities can provide opportunities for habit formation, but smartphone applications can supplement or enhance such opportunities in meaningful ways.

However, the regulatory abilities of adolescents are still developing and may even be impaired in comparison to older children or young adults.[35] What is more, all patience-building activities that *are* effective in adults *are not* necessarily effective in adolescents.[36] Thus, attempts to develop patience interventions targeting adolescents must provide extensive scaffolding as adolescents struggle to regulate their emotions. Smartphones provide contextualized and readily available access to the emotional lives of adolescents, so tech may be an ideal solution for such scaffolding.

Building a Patience App

Recognizing this potential opportunity, our team sought to build a smartphone app that might help adolescents cultivate patience in their daily lives. We assembled an interdisciplinary team composed of members with

33. Schnitker and Emmons, "Patience as a Virtue"; Schnitker, "An Examination of Patience and Well-Being."

34. Schnitker et al., "The Virtue of Patience"; Schnitker et al., "Religion, Spirituality, and Thriving."

35. Smith et al., "Decision Making in Children."

36. Schnitker et al., "Efficacy of Self-Control."

expertise in design, development, personality/social psychology, and developmental psychology. After conducting an extensive review of the scientific literature, our team began an iterative design process whereby we interacted with focus groups with diverse adolescents across multiple timepoints. In our initial conversations, we asked teens to describe real-life scenarios where they struggled with patience, self-control, or regulating emotions. Across the course of subsequent meetings, we solicited adolescent feedback on potential solutions for addressing these felt user needs. After engaging these adolescent focus groups (as well as assessing the app marketplace and reviewing potential designs with multiple stakeholders), we decided to make the development of interpersonal patience the primary focus of the app. In focus groups, adolescents described how they would get stuck in a cycle rehashing the same interpersonal conflicts (or fights, in their language) on a regular basis. They expressed keen interest in an app that would provide them tools for regulating their emotions in these conflicts, which they could use during or immediately after the conflict.

Based on scientifically vetted activities to build patience and emotion regulation, we created a variety of strategies that adolescents could select when they needed help solving a conflict and regulating their emotions. Creating conflict-solving strategies that would be fun, appropriately challenging, short enough for an app, and scientifically sound was no easy task. Whereas the academics on our team had a bias toward content with high fidelity to the scientifically tested intervention protocols, the designer and developer had a bias toward brevity, simplicity, and positive user experience. Only through humble communication and a highly iterative process with feedback from end users (i.e., adolescents) were we able to create tasks that we were confident would build patience and provide an attractive user experience.

The app we developed, named CharacterMe, provided a fairly simple user experience for teens. Adolescents would come to the app with a conflict from their day and choose a strategy to help them deal with it. After choosing a strategy, adolescents were always asked to identify with whom they were having a conflict (from their list of contacts), briefly write what happened, and rate how they felt (i.e., angry, sad, upset, happy) at the worst point of the conflict. Then, they would engage exercises for the specific strategy they chose before ending on a screen that asked them to rate their current feelings.

The specific exercises for each strategy varied in focus and function, but they were all designed to be interactive and based on a previously tested intervention. For example, in the Take Perspective task, teens were asked to rate how the other person felt during the conflict and think about the other person's feelings for one minute (with a countdown timer). In the Mindfulness task, adolescents were given instructions on how to breathe deeply and relax their minds and bodies; then they would practice mindfulness meditation with a countdown timer for various lengths of time. In Selfie, users were asked to take a picture of their face, engage in a quick mindfulness exercise, and then take another picture of their face; this task was designed to increase emotional fluency and awareness. In Listen Up, teens were told to go elsewhere in their phones to listen to a song that would help calm them; a push notification brought them back to the app after several minutes to rate their feelings. Finally, the Think Again task led teens through a series of exercises to help them reappraise, or think differently about, the initial eliciting situation to help them calm themselves.

Users were given points for using strategies and could "level up" when they reached important benchmarks. We chose to include this gamification to make the app more appealing to teens, but we tried to de-emphasize the leveling through the design (e.g., not on every screen, no major "celebration" animation as one moves through levels) in order to avoid producing a product that might increase addictive tendencies. We also included introductory videos that emphasized the intrinsic rewards for the app activities rather than the extrinsic reward of getting more points.

The app was tested in a sample of 516 ethnically and socioeconomically diverse high school students from the greater Los Angeles area (41 percent Asian/Asian American, 30 percent Latinx, 13 percent White, 5 percent Black; 57 percent female). Although data from the app have not been fully analyzed, initial results are promising and show interesting patterns of effects.[37] The various conflict solving strategies differed in their popularity among adolescents. Whereas Mindfulness and ListenUp were the most popular, Selfie and Take Perspective were the least popular. Moreover, the strategies differed in the extent to which users reported reductions in negative emotions or increases in happiness from the worst point of the conflict to post-exercise. Take Perspective and Think Again were more effective than other tasks in reducing feelings of anger, sadness, and upset but less effective in increasing feelings of happiness. Selfie was less effective than

---

37. Schnitker et al., *Context and Framing Effects of a Technology Virtue Intervention.*

other tasks in reducing sadness but more effective in increasing happiness. Mindfulness was less effective than other tasks in reducing upset but more effective in increasing happiness.

Further analyses are needed to assess the efficacy of app use across time, but these initial findings are encouraging. Helping adolescents to be able to regulate their own emotions during or after conflict is a key first step toward building positive relationships. Only once teens (and adults) can regulate their own emotional responses, are they able to really focus on the needs of another person and have the capacity to respond with love. Additional data are needed to see if this or other apps like it can actually change the ways people behave in relational contexts. It is critical that these data are collected on relational outcomes in order to prevent widespread use of a tool that makes users happier at the expense of others. Ultimately, we would want to test how the behaviors of users influence others in their communities such that there is an upward spiral of character development among both users and nonusers.

Moreover, adding features to this or other apps that intend to build patience based on theory and data will improve the ability of these products to affect change. We have plans to better capitalize on the social connection features of smartphones. For instance, after processing a conflict with one of the strategies, users might be offered some text messages they could send to the other person to promote reconciliation. Likewise, the app might be embedded within a youth group or other youth-serving organization such that teens could share some of their conflicts with trained youth leaders, who could then instigate further conversation around how to build patience. These more focused social networking features would allow the technology to promote connection without falling prey to the pitfalls of many social media apps (e.g., excessive self-focus, social comparison). Many adolescents are more comfortable initiating conversations through technology, so providing this technological "entrance" into conversations may increase the frequency of depth of face-to-face interactions between adolescents and their mentors.

The Spirit of Technology

To be clear, a team of psychologists and technologists produced these findings, which means that questions regarding the implications of this research for Christian mission were not made explicit during the course of the study, nor did they serve as the primary impetus for the project. For this very reason, we welcome the critical insights of missiological interlocutors who might be able to help us see what our own disciplinary blinders prevent us from seeing, up to and including rethinking our interpretations of the data and/or reframing our research questions. No doubt, our initial forays—and those of others—need improvement, refinement, or complete revamping.[38]

That being said, a number of theological and, indeed, missiological commitments function as the background conditions for our psychological research and technological development. By explicitly naming a few of these operating assumptions and exploring their most immediate missiological implications, we hope to identify a series of starting points for future collaborations with missiologists that might refine our conceptualizations, elaborate upon our findings, and perhaps even generate new paths of inquiry that are currently unrealized.

The most prominent "theo-logic" that guides our approach not only to research design but also to the application of that research is a fully orbed pneumatology. There is of course a pragmatic rationale for developing virtue interventions through technological means, which is simply that, as stated above, adolescents are overwhelmingly interfacing with their worlds in and through technological means. Some may see this approach as a kind of defeatism or a resigned surrender to the power of technology, and it might very well be if it were pursued in the absence of a robust conception of the Spirit of God in the world. However, one of our basic theological assumptions is that the Trinitarian Spirit of God just is the Spirit of Life who is gratuitously present in the world—the *ruach elohim* who not only breathes life into the whole of the created order, but actively sustains the very existence of the human creature (Psalm 104:29–30). Thus, our prevailing pneumatological concern is not with the essence or origin of the Spirit, but rather with the Spirit's mission in and to the world. In the words of Kirsteen Kim, "The interest today is not so much in philosophy as in the practical questions of how and where the Spirit is to be discerned." What is more, says Kim, "If it is to relate to contemporary society, pneumatology must recognize the Spirit's work beyond the boundaries of the church or the Christian heart."[39]

---

38. Konrath et al., "Can Text Messages Increase Empathy and Prosocial Behavior?"

39. Kim, *The Holy Spirit in the World*, 2–3.

In other words, the strategy of locating character strength interventions where youth are already spending their time reflects a conception of Christian mission that is grounded in a concern with discerning where the Spirit is present in the world and a confident expectation that we will find the Spirit at work beyond the boundaries of the church or the Christian heart—even in the digital spaces created by emerging technologies. This is not to "secularize" or otherwise "demythologize" the work of the Spirit. Nor is it to reduce the Spirit to an entirely internalized experience of the individual or community.[40] It is rather to say that, as the Spirit of life, God is present and active not only in the context of Christian community, but also in and through the underlying structures, systems, and psychologies of a world increasingly driven by techno-cultural change.

Thus, following missiologists like Kim and theologians like Jürgen Moltmann, we are operating with the assumption that creation itself and our life in it are created, structured, and sustained by the presence of the Spirit of God. And if this is the case, then the whole of the created order is not only an in-Spirit-ed site for encountering the Trinitarian God, but it also provides the raw materials with which humans construct their theology of that encounter. Or, as Moltmann puts it,

> According to the biblical traditions, all divine activity is pneumatic in its efficacy. It is always the Spirit who first brings the activity of the Father and the Son to its goal. It follows that the triune God also unremittingly breathes the Spirit into his creation. Everything that is, exists and lives in the unceasing inflow of the energies and potentialities of the cosmic Spirit. This means that we have to understand every created reality in terms of energy, grasping it as the realized potentiality of the divine Spirit. Through the energies and potentialities of the Spirit, the Creator is himself present in his creation. He does not merely confront it in his transcendence; entering into it, he is also immanent in it. The biblical foundation for this interpretation of creation in the Spirit is Psalm 104:29–30.[41]

It therefore follows that, if human technologies (whether a hand-hewn tool or a sophisticated smartphone) are what in-Spirited creatures make of God's in-Spirited creation, then both technological developments and the technologically mediated interactions they occasion are concrete expressions

40. Kim offers a helpful summary of how the "s/Spirit" has often been (mis)understood in theological and missiological discourse, even among Christian theologians. See Kim, *The Holy Spirit in the World*, 24–40.

41. Moltmann, *God in Creation*, 9.

of in-Spirited human creatures collaborating with the Spirit's ongoing creative work in the world. As such, they are not only potential sites for apprehending and responding to the Spirit of life, but they also serve as first-order resources for missiological reflection and engagement.

The Spirit of Patience

Our research indicates that, in formulating an answer to the question of how (and whether) technology both enables and constrains our ability to love the digital other, we would do well to focus our energies on the ways in which the virtue of patience might be cultivated in and through technological means. Although the findings of our study are indeed underwritten by our pneumatological commitments, they are grounded first and foremost in empirical research, which means that, to understand the full weight of their missiological significance, they call for further critical scrutiny. With this in mind, we offer here three potential avenues that might be pursued in order to explore the role that patience plays in missiological engagements with technology.

Patience as a Fundamental Missiological Stance

Participating in the *missio Dei* is as much about the stance we assume toward our neighbors as it is about the criteria we employ for discerning whether the Spirit is, indeed, up to something in our technological interactions with the other (whether religious, political, ethnic, or socioeconomic). To "love our neighbor as ourselves" (Matthew 22: 36–40) implies a certain posture toward our neighbor that cannot be separated from that which constitutes it as an act of love. It is therefore not incidental that Paul's effusive exploration of love in 1 Corinthians 13:4–8 begins with the virtue of patience, almost as if this particular virtue were the necessary precursor for all the others that follow. Cultivating the virtue of patience thus seems to be a kind of gateway, not only to each of the virtues Paul names, but ultimately to the very love that serves as both their origin and telos. In the absence of patience, it is difficult to imagine what kindness or trust or humility or hope would even mean.

The work of Thomàš Halík informs this emphasis on patience as a precondition for missiological engagement. In describing his vision for what Christian witness looks like in the "bustling marketplace of religious wares of every kind," Halík suggests that Christians are called to stand in patient solidarity with cotemporary Zacchaeuses who remain on the sidelines of the Jesus event—curious but noncommittal.[42] "I feel that my chief purpose," says Halík, "is to be an understanding neighbor for those who find it impossible to join the exultant crowds beneath the unfurled flags of whatever color, for those *who keep their distance.*"[43] By framing Christian mission in this way, Halík's concern is not to draw others into the heart of the church, but to broaden that heart by including them.[44]

Adopting this kind of stance toward the religious "other" (which, for Halík, includes the a-/nonreligious other) demands a kind of loving patience that seeks not to move the other from a position of non-belief to belief, but rather to embrace them wherever it is they currently reside, perhaps even indefinitely. The end result is not a conversion of the religious other, but a conversion of the Christian who, by cultivating the virtue of patience, is able to mature in their faith through a newfound capacity to persevere with their doubts and carry non-belief in their hearts. In other words, to adopt a posture of patience is, from a missiological perspective, not principally about giving our religious or nonreligious neighbors the technological means to cultivate their virtue, but first and foremost about "us." It's about being and becoming a people whose love is marked by patience—painstaking, long-suffering, life-giving patience.

Patience Takes Practice

As the saying goes, practice doesn't make perfect; perfect practice makes perfect. The same might be said about cultivating patience with a smartphone. As the findings of our study suggest, incorporating a set of practices into one's daily routine is a critical component of building character strengths, but it is not enough simply to go through the motions provided by a piece of technology (no matter how sophisticated). The reason is because the development of virtue is about more than learning new habits. It's about building a moral identity, which is something that cannot be done in isolation, at least not in any sustainable way. For adolescents in particular, an individual's practices must be embedded within and extended toward a broader network of others in order for these virtue-based practices to be

42. Halík, *Patience with God*, ix.

43. Halík, *Patience with God*, 5 (emphasis in original).

44. Halík, *Patience with God*, 34.

meaningfully taken up as an integral part of their moral identity. And it just so happens that the Christian community—for all its other foibles and failures—is uniquely situated to serve in this lifegiving (and virtue-building) capacity for modern persons, especially those who inhabit an increasingly fragmented, disconnected, and individualized reality.

Indeed, as Warren Brown and Brad Strawn have suggested, the church itself is nothing if not a global network of local communities that are constituted by the extension of individual persons into the larger body of Christ in and through a unique set of physical, embodied practices.[45] Rather than mere habits, these devotional practices are aimed at the development of what Paul calls the fruit of the Spirit (Galatians 5: 22–23)— virtues like love, joy, peace, kindness, and, significantly, patience. In other words, by pressing the question of whether (and how) a virtue like patience might be cultivated in and through technological means, we are not advocating for a disembodied notion of technological innovation, nor a hyper-individualistic approach to Christian mission. If anything, all our data point in the opposite direction—that interpersonal patience might, instead, be cultivated with intentional engagement. This should be an encouragement to psychologists, theologians, and missiologists exploring the various ways in which emerging technologies might facilitate more rather than less in-person interaction.

That being said, our research also suggests that the people-of-God-in-the-world might reconsider what Christian mission looks like in a context increasingly mediated by technology. It may very well be that, in an effort not only to discern but also to participate in the Spirit's ongoing work in the world, one of our most effective strategies in the twenty-first century will be to recommit to what the church has spent the past 2,000 years doing—creating communal spaces for character-building practices that can sustain the formation of one's moral identity.

45. A preliminary version of Brown and Strawn's thoughts in the area of extended cognition can be found in their book *The Physical Nature of Christian Life* and in their forthcoming book, *Supersizing Christian Life*.

Patience as Sabbath Rest

"Recall that you were slaves in the land of Egypt and that the Lord your God brought you out of there by strength and power. That is why the Lord your God has commanded you to observe the Sabbath day."

—Deuteronomy 5:15 (NET)

"For in six days the Lord made the heavens and the earth and the sea and all that is in them, and he rested on the seventh day; therefore the Lord blessed the Sabbath day and set it apart as holy."

—Exodus 20:11 (NET)

In the account found in the book of Deuteronomy, Sabbath keeping is connected to Israel's Exodus from Egypt. Sabbath rest, it would seem, is about more than recovering the energy we expend during the work week. It has something to do with actively resisting the oppressive systems and structures within which we operate. In the Exodus account, however, the rationale for observing the Sabbath is that God rested (Hebrew: *shabath*) on the seventh day of creation (Exodus 20:11). At first blush, this seems to be the opposite of active resistance—a call to cease and desist from whatever activities might be consuming one's time and attention. The theological twist, however, is that sabbath is not a passive verb. It is an active celebration of and delight in God's creation and, subsequently, in what humans make of that creation.

Taken from this perspective, and in light of our study's findings, we might rethink our approach to what a "technological sabbath" entails. Common wisdom would suggest that the best way to develop character strengths in young people is to remove them from the source of their anxiety and inattention (i.e., their smartphones!). But what is actually needed is not so much a break from technology as a mode of sabbath keeping that allows users to actively resist their complicity in technological forms of injustice (e.g., exploitation of information by companies or governments for immoral or materialistic ends, online acts of de-indivualized aggression) and, at the same time, delight in the transformative potential of technological innovations. It is therefore all the more significant that we did not attempt to cultivate the virtue of patience among adolescents by convincing them to abandon their smartphones or to use them less. Instead, we developed an app-based intervention that required users to be actively and intentionally engaged with these ever-present mobile devices, which means that we invited participants to enter into a new kind of relationship with technology—one structured by routinized practices that strategically leverage the benefits of digital technology.

The success of these interventions suggests that emerging approaches to Christian mission might involve the development of technologically mediated forms of sabbath keeping that are designed to celebrate the deliverances of technology rather than dissuade people from using tools that are otherwise integral to their daily lives. For sabbath rest, much like patience, is not about engaging in a pious kind of "do-nothing-ness," or removing ourselves entirely from the urgent demands of an otherwise harried and impatient world we have no capacity to resist. Just as patience is not simply an ability to wait passively until things get better, but an active willingness to suffer, tolerate, and bear the weight of difficult circumstances, sabbath keeping is an active form of intentionally delighting in the goodness of God's creation in the midst of a cultural context that would have us do otherwise.[46]

Conclusion

Echoing Karl Barth, it is important to keep in mind the yes in our no and the no in our yes.[47] More specifically, our enthusiasm for the missiological potential of technologically mediated virtue interventions should not be mistaken for an uncritical embrace of all things technological. Our "yes" to technology is a qualified affirmation. But if our empirical research is a trustworthy barometer (and we think it is), and if our pneumatological commitments are sound (and we think they are), then we need not be overly concerned about saying "no" to technology. In fact, we would go one step further and say that we can confidently affirm those technologies that help adolescents cultivate virtues like patience. Or, to put it somewhat differently, the yes embedded in our no involves what is potentially a radical embrace of technologies that provide us with new and emerging means for loving our (digital) neighbors in a digitally networked society.

46. Schnitker et al., "The Virtue of Patience, Spirituality, and Suffering."
47. Barth, *The Epistle to the Romans.*

Bibliography

Anderson, Craig, and Brad J. Bushman. "Effects of Violent Video Games on Aggressive Behavior, Aggressive Cognition, Aggressive Affect, Physiological Arousal, and Prosocial Behavior: A Meta-Analytic Review of the Scientific Literature." *Psychological Science* 12.5 (2001) 353–59.

Anderson, Monica, and Jingiing Jiang. "Teens, Social Media & Technology 2018." *Pew Research* (June 2018). http://publicservicesalliance.org/wp-content/uploads/2018/06/Teens-Social-Media-Technology-2018-PEW.pdf.

Barth, Karl. *The Epistle to the Romans*. 6th ed. Translated by Edwyn C. Hoskyns. New York: Oxford University Press, 1968.

Brown, Warren S., and Brad D. Strawn. *The Physical Nature of Christian Life*. New York: Cambridge University Press, 2012.

———. *Supersizing Christian Life*. Downer's Grove, IL: InterVarsity, 2020.

Buffardi, Laura, and W. Keith Campbell. "Narcissism and Social Networking Web Sites." *Personality and Social Psychology Bulletin* 34.10 (2008) 1303–14.

Business Wire. "Where Does the Time Go? Timex Releases Results of Survey Detailing How Americans Spend Their Time." *BusinessWire.com*, September 25, 2012. https://www.businesswire.com/news/home/20120925006167/en/Time-Timex-Releases-Results-Survey-Detailing-Americans.

Carden, Lucas, and Wendy Wood. "Habit Formation and Change." *Current Opinion in Behavioral Sciences* 20 (2018) 117–22.

Common Sense Media. "The Common Sense Census: Media Use by Tweens and Teens." Common Sense Media, 2015. https://www.commonsensemedia.org/sites/default/files/uploads/research/census_executivesummary.pdf.

Halík, Thomàš. *Patience with God: The Story of Zacchaeus Continuing in Us*. New York: Doubleday, 2009.

Harned, David Bailey. *Patience: How We Wait upon the World*. Cambridge, MA: Cowley, 1997.

Kim, Kirsteen. *The Holy Spirit in the World: A Global Conversation*. New York: Orbis, 2007.

Konrath, Sara, Emily Falk, Andrea Fuhrel-Forbis, Mary Liu, James E. Swain, Richard Tolman, Rebecca Cunningham, and Maureen Walton. "Can Text Messages Increase Empathy and Prosocial Behavior? The Development and Initial Validation of Text to Connect." 2015. PLOS ONE 10(9) e0137585. https://doi.org/10.1371/journal.pone.0137585.

Korea Internet and Security Agency. *2016 Survey on Internet Usage*. Seoul, Korea: Internet and Security Agency, 2017.

Krasnova, Hanna, Helena Wenninger, Thomas Widjaja, and Peter Buxmann. "Envy on Facebook: A Hidden Threat to Users' Life Satisfaction?" February 2013. Proceedings of the 11th International Conference on Wirtschaftsinformatik, Leipzig, Germany.

Lally, Phillippa, Cornelia H. M. Van Jaarsveld, Henry W. W. Potts, and Jane Wardle. "How Are Habits Formed: Modelling Habit Formation in the Real World." *European Journal of Social Psychology* 40.6 (2010) 998–1009.

Lavelock, Caroline R., Everett L. Worthington, Brandon J. Griffin, A. H. Cairo, and Sarah A. Schnitker. "Good Things Come to Those Who (Peacefully) Wait." Manuscript submitted for publication, 2019.

Logistics at MGEPS at UPV. "How Much Time of an Average Life Is Spent Waiting?" April 4, 2017. https://logisticsmgepsupv.wordpress.com/2017/04/04/how-much-time-of-an-average-life-is-spent-waiting/.

Misra, Shalini, Lulu Cheng, Jamie Genevie, and Miao Yuan. "The iPhone Effect: The Quality of In-Person Social Interactions in the Presence of Mobile Devices." *Environment & Behavior* 48.2 (2016) 275–98. doi:10.1177/0013916514539755C.

Moltmann, Jürgen. *God in Creation: A New Theology of Creation and the Spirit of God.* Translated by Margaret Kohl. Minneapolis: Fortress, 1993.

Murray, Janet H. *Hamlet on the Holodeck: The Future of Narrative in Cyberspace.* New York: Free, 1997.

Nesi, Jacqueline, and Mitchell Prinstein. "Using Social Media for Social Comparison and Feedback-Seeking: Gender and Popularity Moderate Associations with Depressive Symptoms." *Journal of Abnormal Child Psychology* 43.8 (2015) 1427–38.

Oxford University Press. "Patience." *Oxford English Dictionary Online.* http://www.oxforddictionaries.com/us/definition/american_english/patience.

Pew Research Center. "Smartphone Ownership and Internet Usage Continues to Climb in Emerging Economies." *Pew Research Center*, February 22, 2016. http://www.pewglobal.org/2016/02/22/smartphone-ownership-and-internet-usage-continues-to-climb-in-emerging-economies/.

Przybylski, Andrew, and Netta Weinstein. "Can You Connect with Me Now? How the Presence of Mobile Communication Technology Influences Face-to-Face Conversation Quality." *Journal of Social and Personal Relationships* 30.3 (2013) 237–46.

Rorty, Amélie. *Essays on Aristotle's Ethics.* Berkeley, CA: University of California Press, 1980.

Rosen, L. D., K. Whaling, S. Rab, L. M. Carrier, N. A. Cheever. "Is Facebook Creating 'iDisorders'? The Link Between Clinical Symptoms of Psychiatric Disorders and Technology Use, Attitudes and Anxiety." *Computers in Human Behavior* 29.3 (2013) 1243–54.

Schnitker, Sarah. "An Examination of Patience and Well-Being." *Journal of Positive Psychology* 7.4 (2012) 263–80. doi:10.1080/17439760.2012.697185.

———, and Robert Emmons. "Patience as a Virtue: Religious and Psychological Perspectives." *Research in the Social Scientific Study of Religion* 18 (2007) 177–207. doi:10.1163/ej.9789004158511.i-301.69.

———, Thomas J. Felke, Justin L. Barrett, and Robert A. Emmons. "Longitudinal Study of Religious and Spiritual Transformation in Adolescents Attending Young Life Summer Camp: Assessing the Epistemic, Intrapsychic, and Moral Sociability Functions of Conversion." *Psychology of Religion and Spirituality* 6.2 (2014) 83–93.

———, Thomas. J. Felke, Nathaniel A. Fernandez, Nanyamka Redmond, and Amber E. Blews. "Efficacy of Self-Control and Patience Interventions in Adolescents." *Applied Developmental Science* 21.3 (2017) 165–83. doi: 10.1080/10888691.2016.1178578.

———, Benjamin Houltberg, William Dyrness, and Nanyamka Redmond. "The Virtue of Patience, Spirituality, and Suffering: Integrating Lessons from Positive Psychology, Psychology of Religion, and Christian Theology." *Psychology of Religion and Spirituality* 9.3 (2017) 264–75. http://dx.doi.org/10.1037/rel0000099.

———, Benjamin Houltberg, Jennifer Shubert, and Lixian Cui. *Context and Framing Effects of a Technology Virtue Intervention.* Unpublished raw dataset (January 2019).

———, Pamela King, and Benjamin Houltberg. "Religion, Spirituality, and Thriving: Transcendent Narrative, Virtue, and Telos." *Journal of Research on Adolescence* 29 (2019) 276–90. doi:10.1111/jora.12443.

———, Diana B. Ro, Joshua D. Foster, Alexis D. Abernethy, Joseph M. Currier, Charlotte vanOyen Witvliet, Lindsey M. Root Luna, Katharine M. Putman, Karl VanHarn, and Janet Carter. "Patient Patients: Increased Patience Associated with Decreased Depressive Symptoms in Psychiatric Treatment." *The Journal of Positive Psychology* 15.3 (2020) 300–313. doi: 10.1080/17439760.2019.1610482.

Schueller, Stephen M., Ricardo F. Muñoz, and David C. Mohr. "Realizing the Potential of Behavioral Intervention Technologies." *Current Directions in Psychological Science* 22.6 (2013) 478–83.

Smith, Dana G., Lin Xiao, and Antoine Bechara. "Decision Making in Children and Adolescents: Impaired Iowa Gambling Task Performance in Early Adolescence." *Developmental Psychology* 48.8 (2012) 1180–88.

Smith, James K. A. *You Are What You Love: The Spiritual Power of Habit.* Grand Rapids: Brazos, 2016.

Thomas, R. M., and Sarah Schnitker. "Modeling the Effects of Within-Person Characteristic and Goal-Level Attributes on Personal Project Pursuit Over Time." *Journal of Research in Personality* 69 (2017) 206–17. doi:10.1016/j.jrp.2016.06.012

Turkle, Sherry. *Alone Together: Why We Expect More from Technology and Less from Each Other.* New York: Basic, 2011.

Twenge, Jean M. *iGen: Why Today's Super-Connected Kids Are Growing Up Less Rebellious, More Tolerant, Less Happy—and Completely Unprepared for Adulthood—and What That Means for the Rest of Us.* New York: Atria, 2018.

Van Deursen, Alexander J. A. M., Colin L. Bolle, Sabrina M. Begner, and Piet A. M. Kommers. "Modeling Habitual and Addictive Smartphone Behavior: The Role of Smartphone Usage Types, Emotional Intelligence, Social Stress, Self-Regulation, Age, and Gender." *Computers in Human Behavior* 45 (2015) 411–20.

Wright, N. T. *After You Believe: Why Christian Character Matters.* New York: HarperOne, 2010.

CHAPTER 6

The Quest to Become More Human

Christian Witness & the Transhumanist Movement

ANGELA WILLIAMS GORRELL

Transhumanism is a modern-day philosophical and cultural movement being articulated and developed primarily by philosophers, technologists, and futurists. Transhumanists are offering visions of a life worth living that are having a massive impact on what technologies are being created and for what purposes—technologies that will likely impact your life, my life, and the lives of generations after us. It is important to examine transhumanist visions of a good life and how such visions have been formed in order to explore the shape of Christian witness in our current and forthcoming technological landscape.

Similar to people from other philosophical and religious traditions—Christian and otherwise—transhumanists have convictions about human beings and the world as well as hopes regarding what humans ought to be seeking, valuing, and doing in order to have a good life. "Transhumanism seeks more than merely new technological gadgets. It seeks to construct a philosophy of life, a total worldview, a grand metanarrative," writes systematic theologian Ted Peters.[1] Transhumanism is not value-free.[2] Transhumanist values, beliefs, and aspirations are being backed by billions of dollars and therefore, transhumanist visions of the good life are impacting healthcare, economics, and public policies.

1. Peters, "Progress and Provolution," 66.
2. Peters, "Progress and Provolution," 75.

There are in fact Christian transhumanists, people who are passionate about using technology ethically to partner with God to accomplish God's work in the world.[3] Christian transhumanists view using medical interventions to enhance or sustain physical life as divinely inspired healing work or the attainment of immortality as God's gift of eternal life (in a form we did not quite understand until now). The Christian Transhumanist Association has a list of affirmations that includes the call to love their neighbor and work against hunger, illness, and death; their desire for progress and growth, and recognition of science and technology as goods that nurture expressions of the *imago Dei*.[4] The Christian Transhumanist Association believes that technology coupled with following Christ will enable them to become more human.[5]

The affirmations of Christian transhumanists are good and it is important to imagine common goals Christians and transhumanists could work on together, such as responding meaningfully to suffering or eliminating the possibility of nuclear war. At the same time, a close examination of transhumanist statements elucidates important distinctions between truth claims, values, and hopes of the transhumanist movement and truth claims, values, and hopes within the historic Christian tradition. Transhumanist visions of a life worth living are different than Christian visions of a life worth living.

Given that the transhumanist movement is still gathering momentum and every movement (or tradition) has *visions*, rather than a vision, and such visions are always varied and dynamic, the transhumanist picture I describe will inevitably be incomplete. It is also essential to realize that not all transhumanists have the same goals or believe the same things, similar to people from various denominations within Christianity. However, assessing particular aspirations, claims, and principles of specific leaders within the transhumanist movement is beneficial for understanding the dynamics of our technological landscape, how people's lives are being and could be impacted by such dynamics, and how Christians might influence the design, development, use, transformation, or rejection of particular technologies through embodied Christian witness in a technological age.

---

3. Miller, "Should we live to be 500?"

4. Christian Transhumanist Association, "The Christian Transhumanist Affirmation."

5. Christian Transhumanist Association, "The Christian Transhumanist Affirmation."

Transhumanist Visions of a Good Life

The goal of Humanity+, the leading organization of the contemporary transhumanist movement, is for "people to be better than well."[6] Transhumanists advocate "for the well-being of all sentience in whatever form that it takes now and in the future."[7] Transhumanists define well-being in particular ways, ultimately promoting projects and technologies that expand human intellectual and physiological capacities with the hope of eventually ending involuntary suffering and aging.[8]

Transhumanist ideals and ethics are heavily influenced by two philosophical traditions: utilitarianism and Nietzschean philosophy, though some transhumanists align more with one tradition than the other. Leading transhumanist and philosopher Nick Bostrom, for example, contends that transhumanists have more in common with utilitarianism than Nietzsche.[9] Utilitarianism is a philosophical tradition and ethical theory that is consequentialist. Therefore, morality and good decision-making are purely related to the consequences they produce. In his seminal work *Utilitarianism*, John Stuart Mill (drawing on the scholarship of Jeremy Bentham) proposes that the right action is an action that provides maximum happiness for the greatest number of people and simultaneously limits the most suffering.[10] Classical utilitarianism, otherwise known as hedonistic utilitarianism, defines such happiness as the presence of pleasure and absence of pain.[11] Utilitarian understandings about right action and happiness have influenced transhumanist visions of human flourishing and the technological development that is informed by such visions.

In fact, a model of transhumanism, identified as postsuffering transhumanism or abolitionism, illuminates connections between values of hedonistic utilitarianism and transhumanism.[12] Postsuffering transhumanism developed around David Pearce's manifesto, "The Hedonistic Imperative," focuses on accomplishing the end of sentient suffering and a time when

6. Humanity+, "Humanity+—What We Do."

7. Humanity+, "Transhumanist Declaration."

8. Humanity+, "Humanity+—What We Do." See also H+Pedia, "Transhumanist Bill of Rights."

9. Bostrom, "A History of Transhumanist Thought," 4–5.

10. Mill, *Utilitarianism*, 9–10.

11. Sinnott-Armstrong, "Consequentialism."

12. Pearce, "The Abolitionist Project."

sentient beings live forever with limitless happiness and leisure.[13] David Pearce is the co-founder of Humanity+. The kind of circumstances transhumanists like Pearce advocate for are ones in which all forms of unpleasant experience are abolished. In Humanity+'s explanation of why people would want to live forever, happiness is a central concern. The organization writes, "The goal is more healthy, happy, productive years. Ideally, everybody should have the right to choose when and how to die—or not to die. Transhumanists want to live longer because they want to do, learn, and experience more; have more fun and spend more time with loved ones."[14]

While Bostrom contends that transhumanism is more aligned with utilitarianism than Nietzschean ideals, other prominent transhumanists like futurist and philosopher Max More and philosopher Stefan Lorenz Sorgner see significant similarities between the concept of the *posthuman* and Nietzsche's concept of the overhuman. "Certainly there is no inconsistency between transhumanism and a utilitarian morality. But neither is there any inconsistency between transhumanism and a more Nietzschean view of morality," writes Max More.[15] Importantly, More has also written, "Although there are clear parallels between Nietzsche's thinking and some core transhumanist ideas, the latter are inspired *very selectively* by the former."[16]

Just as some transhumanists draw from particular aspects of utilitarianism like increasing pleasure and reducing pain, abolishing suffering, and/or lifting up actions that provide maximum happiness for the greatest number of people while simultaneously limiting the most suffering, other transhumanists focus particularly on Nietzsche's concept of the *will to power*.

Nietzsche believed the fundamental instinct of life is the expansion of power. In other words, for Nietzsche the great and small human struggle always revolves around superiority, growth and expansion, and power.[17] The key to the good life for Nietzsche was becoming an overcomer by embracing one's power, individuality, and freedom. Given this, Peters illuminates a significant tension in the transhumanist movement between utilitarian and Nietzchean principles, writing, "Transhumanist ethics is torn by a tension between the capitalist values adhering to the survival-of-the-fittest principle

13. Pearce, "The Hedonistic Imperative."

14. Humanity+, "Transhumanist FAQ."

15. More, "The Overhuman in the Transhuman," 1–4.

16. More, "The Overhuman in the Transhuman," 1.

17. Nietzsche, *The Gay Science*, 27, 163.

and the altruistic values of a benevolent community."[18] The influence of both utilitarian and Nietzschean philosophy as well as the potential for conflict becomes evident when examining aspirations and values of specific leaders within the transhumanist movement.

Aspirations and Values

In "Transhumanism," the evolutionary biologist Julian Huxley describes the importance of *enhancing humanity* through exploring human nature and its possibilities, as Huxley believed the most vital aim for humankind is the fullest realization of human beings' possibilities.[19] Like Huxley believed in the mid-1950s, Humanity+ members also "believe that humanity's potential is still mostly unrealized. There are possible scenarios that lead to wonderful and exceedingly worthwhile enhanced human conditions."[20] Huxley out-lines principles grounded in reason that he feels support the ideal of human enhancement through the maximization of human possibility. For example, beauty is indispensable and ugliness is therefore immoral, though both the content of Huxley's perception of beauty and immorality and how he came to the conclusion that beauty is indispensable is unclear.

Huxley contends that enhancement requires that the quality of people should eclipse the quantity of them. Similarly, philosopher Jonathan Glover explains in *What Sort of People Should there Be?* that only certain elements of human nature are worth maintaining—features especially that contribute to self-development and self-expression, to certain kinds of relationships, and to the development of human consciousness and understanding.[21] The prefix *trans* when combined with the word *human* suggests that what humans need to do is to *go beyond* or *change thoroughly* our current con-dition. Contemporary transhumanists want human beings to focus on realizing our full potential through "fundamentally improving the human condition" psychologically, intellectually and physically.[22] Transhuman-ists believe human enhancement and improvement is especially possible through a reliance on critical reason, science, and technology.

18. Peters, "Progress and Provolution," 72.

19. Huxley, *New Bottles*, 13 (emphasis added).

20. Humanity+, "Transhumanist Declaration."

21. Glover, *What Sort of People Should There Be?*

22. Sorgner, "Transhumanism."

Transhumanists describe the importance of dependence on applied reason and science to make personal decisions about which aspects of a person's mind and body should be enhanced.[23] For transhumanists, determining the aspects of humanity that will nurture self-development, self-realization, and self-expression involves careful deliberation of risks and opportunities and beneficial applications.[24] Humanity+ describes using applied reasoning and knowledge through observation in terms of research, forums, education, discussion, public debate, critical thinking, artistic exploration, and, potentially, cognitive enhancers.[25]

In order to end unchosen suffering and aging, transhumanists believe humans need to use critical reason and scientific evidence to discover technological solutions for becoming a stronger species—cognitively and physiologically. Bostrom explains, "Transhumanists emphasize the enormous potential for *genuine improvements* in human well-being and human flourishing that are attainable *only via technological transformation*."[26] Similarly, Humanity+ has a Transhumanist Declaration, which explains, "Humanity stands to be profoundly affected by science and technology in the future. We envision the possibility of broadening human potential by overcoming aging, cognitive shortcomings, involuntary suffering, and our confinement to planet Earth."[27] In sum, transhumanist visions of the good life are focused on self-transformation and improvement through technological solutions.

Technologies are currently being developed that will considerably lengthen people's lifetimes and help people to feel better and be healthier for more years of their lives. Some of the possibilities are related to genetics, like gene modification and genetic fortune telling. Other possibilities are connected to the design and development of robotic parts (e.g., limbs, custom-made organs) or storing organs for transplantation. An extreme version of storage is cryonics, "an effort to save lives by using temperatures so cold that a person beyond help by today's medicine can be preserved for decades or centuries until a future medical technology can restore that person to full health."[28] There are also emerging technologies like nano-

---

23. Humanity+, "Transhumanist FAQ."

24. Bostrom, "Human Genetic Enhancements," 499.

25. Humanity+, "Transhumanist FAQ." See also their "Transhumanist Declaration."

26. Bostrom, "A History of Transhumanist Thought," 20.

27. Humanity+, "Transhumanist Declaration."

28. ACLOR Life Extension Foundation, "What is Cryonics?"

technology that could change the way food is made and the way people get nutrients and energy to live. The idea is to provide optimum nutrition for longevity. In addition to using technology to prolong human lifespans, Transhumanists desire to lessen global warming and protect animals (which support human life) and also support space travel and anything else that will contribute to longer lives.[29]

Indeed, technology, improvement, and self-transformation have a role in living a good life. As Peters comments, "What I like about the technoenthusiasts among us is the unapologetic extravagance of their vision. I like their zeal for transformation. I like their celebration of the new."[30] However, while technology, improvement, and self-transformation can contribute to human flourishing, each in its own way can also become an impediment to human flourishing. Technology is sometimes developed and used for damaging purposes and thus can contribute to malign circumstances, harmful practices, and destructive feelings. Also, improvement is often ambiguous, lacking guiding principles, which can nurture insecurity and anxiety. And fixating on self-transformation can cause an obsessive turn inward that then nurtures fear of rejection, loneliness, and negative social comparison. Importantly, technological solutions, improvement, and self-transformation can thwart our efforts to live the true life when they are not directed toward a meaningful purpose.

Christian Witness

Transhumanists are encouraging and supporting well-being, freedom of choice, the reduction of suffering and aging, and the end of death. In view of this, embodying an alternative vision of human flourishing in our current and forthcoming technological landscape means doing careful critical and theological work and being cautious that Christian witness does not involve promoting suffering or death. In fact, inventor and futurist Ray Kurzweil critiques religion for this very thing, writing, "The primary role of traditional religion is deathist rationalization—that is, rationalizing the tragedy of death as a good thing."[31]

Powerful Christian witness in our current and forthcoming technological landscape is and will be life-affirming. There are many ways Christian

---

29. H+Pedia, "Transhumanist Bill of Rights."

30. Peters, "Progress and Provolution," 64.

31. Kurzweil, *The Singularity Is Near*, 372.

witness can be life-affirming while remaining committed to Christian be-liefs, values, and practices. Practical theologian Michael Stroope helpfully clarifies what Christian witness requires:

> *Witness* is not a synonym for *persuasion, argument,* or *coercion.* Witness runs in two directions, each compounding the other. Wit-ness is both beholding and telling. To *behold* is to witness some-thing that changes one's existence. Beholding is more than seeing with physical eyes; it is to be captured by a vision. . . . To *tell* is to do more than recount events with a line of argument or in a dispassionate manner; rather, *telling* is to convey with one's words *and life* what has been seen and experienced.[32]

Reflecting on aims and desires of the transhumanist movement al-lows me to explore characteristics of *beholding* and *telling* in six main areas: meaningful ends, the body, suffering, inequality, technology design, and "interested conversation."[33] It is essential to consider the significance of Christian witness in the development and use of new technologies and par-ticularly what your community's witness might look like.

Meaningful Ends

In a technological landscape fixated on means, a key characteristic of power-ful, life-affirming Christian witness is passionate investment in and personal concern with meaningful ends. Christian witness involves invitations to think about the ultimate aim of all of our endeavors, especially our techno-logical transformations. Rather than being focused on human enhancement, Christians witness to the hope of becoming more *fully human*, a quest exem-plified in the life and teachings of Jesus. In *always on*, I explore diminished humanness, the chief challenge of our new media landscape.[34] American novelist and activist James Baldwin writes that what human beings believe, do, and cause others to endure testifies to their inhumanity and fear.[35] The shape of Christian witness in a technological era must be informed by a de-sire for words and deeds that testify to our *humanity*. In order to endeavor to

---

32. Stroope, *Transcending Mission,* 371 (emphasis original).

33. Gorrell, *always on,* 11.

34. Gorrell, *always on,* 20.

35. Baldwin, "The Fire Next Time," and "My Dungeon Shook," 293, in *Collected Essays.*

become fully human, Christian communities do not simply explore human nature, but the nature of God.

Christian communities attempt to understand God in light of the life and ministry of Jesus. Jesus' life and teachings are the prevailing norm. Christian communities behold and tell that "the image of God in all its fullness has been revealed and restored in Jesus Christ, in whom we find our true humanity" (2 Corinthians 4:4; Colossians 1:15).[36] Jesus is the key to human existence. Jesus' life and teachings illustrated the good life as a life "rooted in God's character as universal, unconditional, and omnipotent love," writes systematic theologian Miroslav Volf and New Testament scholar Matthew Croasmun.[37] The source of Jesus' identity was God's unchanging, unconditional, relentless love. Jesus' teachings invite humans to reflect on, abide in, and participate in God's love (e.g. John 15:1–17). Love is a true telos. Love is not a means. Love should not be instrumentalized, rather it is an ultimate end that we should be oriented by and live toward.

Meaning and purpose is found in experiencing and sharing in God's love. Christians witness, as Jesus did, to God's love by the way they allow this love to transform their being, their words and deeds, and the way they see and relate to others, themselves (including their bodies), God, and creation—in short, in the way they live.[38] In order to learn about and become rooted in God's love, Christians participate in community where Christians engage in social practices, unified by their effort to proclaim and be disciples of God's Word and thus Jesus (Ephesians 4).[39] Christian communities are a sort of family with people of very different classes and circumstances, that have an abiding reference point for the direction of their lives whether in or out of such Christian company.[40] Christian communities witness to God's love by their altered social relations not just with one another, but with people beyond the community as "God's kingdom is manifested in the concrete forms in which social relationships are practiced."[41]

---

36. Volf and Croasmun, *For the Life of the World*, 16.

37. Volf and Croasmun, *For the Life of the World*, 72–73.

38. Volf and Croasmun, *For the Life of the World*, 72–73.

39. Tanner, *Theories of Culture*, 136, 152.

40. Tanner, *Theories of Culture*, 98.

41. Shenk, *The Transfiguration of Mission*, 86. See also Tanner, *Theories of Culture*, 103.

The teachings of Jesus reveal that an action is good if it is related to loving God and loving others (Mark 12:30–31), which is not necessarily an action that will bring pleasure instead of pain or is beneficial for the most people, or is correlated with weighing risks and opportunities. Instead, Christian communities witness are guided by love, which sometimes calls for engaging in social practices and participating in altered social relationships in digital and physical spaces that are inconvenient, even costly. Christian communities witness that a life worth living is not necessarily life going well in the form of happiness, productivity, or longevity; rather the good life crucially bears distinctive, nourishing, meaningful fruit of the Spirit: love, joy, peace, patience, kindness, goodness, faithfulness, gentleness, and self-control (Galatians 5:22–23).

Whereas transhumanist visions of self-transformation involve achieving one's intellectual and physical potential and thus fixation on the self, being rooted in God's love nurtures self-transcendence. God's love looks like reaching out beyond the self, back toward God and out toward others, and recognizing interconnectedness with God, others, and creation (see Genesis 2; John 1; 1 Corinthians 12:12–14; 1 John 4:7–16). Self-transcendence also draws attention to the importance not just of the psychological, intellectual, and physical dimensions of people's lives that transhumanists focus on transforming, but also to the *relational* and *spiritual* aspects of humanity.[42] Additionally, Christians behold and tell that means like technological solutions, improvement, and self-transformation, if utilized or pursued, need to be directed toward our ultimate aim of becoming fully human like Jesus, which looks like living toward and embodying God's love and thus nurturing self-transcendence. Ultimately, Christians witness to the significance of what humans seek, that what we orient our lives toward matters deeply.

The Body

Aiming for improvement and self-transformation without love as an ultimate concern often adds to suffering rather than eliminating it. Valuing improvement and self-transformation without love will likely contribute to further classification, categorization, comparison, and competition between human beings, all of which can be linked to injustice, oppression, and often, forms of cruelty. Transhumanist visions of the good life raise important concerns

42. Zimmermann, "Human Flourishing in a Technological World."

about the human body and questions about what constitutes a human being. Therefore, Christian witness in a technological age also includes attentiveness to the integrated human being, affirmation of the dignity of all bodies, and appreciation for the diversity in human forms.

Contemporary transhumanists want human beings to focus on realizing our full potential through "fundamentally improving the human condition psychologically, intellectually and physically."[43] However, Christian communities witness with their deeds and words to the nature and significance of the *integrated self*, a self with intellectual, psychological, and physical dimensions, but also a self with emotional, social, and spiritual dimensions.

One extreme option some transhumanists imagine related to using technology to prolong human life is to download the content of human brains to machines so that people's bodies can deteriorate, but their minds can live on.[44] People who imagine such options appear to have a limited understanding of what constitutes a human. Ethicist Devan Stahl points out, "Transhumanist discourse seems radically out of touch with phenomenological, feminist, black, disability, and other discourses, which stress the importance of the body as central to identity formation."[45] Humans are not merely beings with consciousness. Philosopher and theologian Jens Zimmerman, co-leader of a significant project reflecting on human flourishing in a technological age, rightly contends, "The whole living human being is a *person*: human subjectivity is a totality, characterized by an embodied, socially constituted, historical, self-reflexive awareness of and relation to the world and others."[46] Christian witness that is life-affirming values every dimension of personhood.

Aspirations of enhancing humanity (or human possibility) and ending involuntary suffering and aging could easily encourage preference for particular kinds of able-bodiedness and intellectual capacity, veneration of youthfulness as well as an underlying disdain for human frailties, and an indifference to one's own body.[47] With improvement and self-transformation as primary, human beings can easily be viewed as *projects* rather

---

43. Sorgner, "Transhumanism."

44. Angelica, ed., *The Ray Kurzweil Reader*, 81–86. See also Kurzweil, *The Singularity Is Near*.

45. Stahl, "Tillich and Transhumanism," 191.

46. Zimmermann, "Human Flourishing" (emphasis original).

47. O'Connell, "600 Miles in a Coffin-Shaped Bus."

than sites of the living God—birthplaces for an encounter with meaning, beauty, truth, goodness, the divine. [48] Practical theologian John Swinton encourages, "As we gaze upon our different bodies, rather than assuming that there is a need for healing and change, either now or in the future, we can recognize each one is a site of holiness and a place of meeting."[49] In view of Swinton's convictions, another feature of being life-affirming in our current and forthcoming landscape is recognizing that the uniqueness of each person is a gift from God and affirming the dignity of and light within all people—without favoritism for particular abilities, mental or emotional health statuses, or intellectual capacities.

Appreciation for differently abled bodies is crucial for recognizing that "human bodies and human disability have meanings that stretch beyond our simplistic biomedical assumptions that we need to fix what is broken and normalise what we consider to be abnormal."[50] Such appreciation requires reflection on the deeper meaning behind human diversity as well as what society views as normal, especially intellectually, physically, and psychologically. Therefore, another characteristic of Christian witness in relationship to the human body is appreciation of the diversity of human beings, diversity that occurs in a multiplicity of ways, through social practices like truth-telling, celebration, gratitude, hospitality, and friendship. Notably, appreciating differences in humans does not preclude Christians from meaningfully responding to suffering. It is a false choice to imagine that Christians cannot witness to the importance of affirming and appreciating the diversity in human forms while also participating in reducing suffering, a main aim of the transhumanist movement.

Suffering

Another facet of being life-affirming in our current and forthcoming landscape is for Christian witness to testify to the sources of suffering and the sources of holistic healing. Transhumanists who are affiliated with Humanity+ recognize that "Inequity, discrimination, and stigmatization—against or on behalf of modified people—could become serious issues."[51] They have

48. Cole-Turner, "Introduction," 7 (emphasis added), in Cole-Turner, ed., *Transhumanism and Transcendence*.

49. Swinton, "Many Bodies, Many Worlds," 23.

50. Swinton, "Many Bodies, Many Worlds," 20.

51. Humanity+, "Transhumanist FAQ."

proposed solutions like "fostering a climate of tolerance and acceptance towards those who are different from ourselves" and strengthening "institutions that prevent violence and protect human rights." However, these proposals neglect the above-mentioned tensions between utilitarian and Nietzschean morality as well as sin.

Christian communities recognize human beings' propensity to sin—to be guided by destructive ideologies and human activities that stem from ignorance, immaturity, and indecency and are fueled by disgust, entitlement, pride, greed, and other *diseases of the soul*. From a Christian perspective, human beings have broken relations with creation, others, God, and our embodied self. When we do not practice unconditional love and instead live for ourselves and become content with malfunctioning or destroyed connections to creation, others, God, or even our embodied self (e.g., as displayed in self-harm), our deeds and words contribute to pain and suffering in the world. Simply wanting to foster the right kind of climate or strengthening institutions is not enough, as history demonstrates. Christian witness highlights the need for the Spirit, for the very being of God, to heal humans and help us to be people of love, rather than people who minimize the humanity of ourselves and others. Christian communities testify to God's grace and mercy by acknowledging the way we contribute to suffering, taking responsibility for suffering we cause, confessing wrongdoing, and repenting.

By the grace of God, Christian communities can listen for and respond to the Spirit's leading and live from the Spirit's power, witnessing to the significance of living for others and participating in God's unconditional love. Such participation often takes the form of breaking cycles of violence through forgiving, loving enemies, lamenting with those who are mourning, and active peacebuilding.[52] Practical theologian Bryan Stone writes, "Our task as Christians is to better learn how to clarify and exemplify our ridiculous hope so that it can be recognized as good news. Ultimately that will mean corporately embodying this hope as a distinctive people—living before the world as people of promise and peace."[53]

Transhumanists and Christians can agree that eliminating unnecessary forms of suffering is meaningful, essential work. Christian witness demonstrates that technological solutions are one way to meaningfully respond to suffering, but there are other ways too. It is also important for

52. Gorrell, *always on*, 93.

53. Stone, *Evangelism after Pluralism*, 81.

Christian witness to demonstrate that we must address suffering in its various forms. Throughout his ministry, Jesus heals not only people's bodies, but also how people are seen by their communities and themselves, as well as the broken relationships and circumstances in which people are entangled. Christian witness demonstrates attending to suffering by being present to and even sometimes sharing in other people's suffering. Throughout Jesus' ministry, he constantly recognized, embraced, listened to, and got close to people who were suffering.

Part of loving other people well is testifying to their pain, by acknowledging it as such and allowing others to express their pain without interruption and without the need to immediately respond with solutions—especially when such pain is emotional, relational, systemic, or generational. To behold and share space with and share in another's suffering is to embody genuine compassion. Witnessing to someone else's suffering and attending to it with deep listening and mercy is part of the practice of holistic healing, healing that lessens the burden of suffering and its capacity for isolating the sufferer by empathizing with suffering. Christian communities witness with their deeds and words, as Jesus did, to the power of holistic healing.

Inequality

If human beings begin to significantly modify their minds and bodies in order to enhance their intellectual capacities or live longer lives, worse inequality is another major concern. There are transhumanists like Bostrom who outright admit that inequality is and will continue to be a given.[54] Bostrom explains that transhumanists "accept a wide range of inequalities" because they are "deserved, have social benefits, or are unavoidable concomitants to free individuals making their own and sometimes foolish choices about how to live their lives" and believe an "increase in unjust inequalities due to technology is not a sufficient reason for discouraging the development and use of the technology."[55] In light of this, another facet of being life-affirming is for Christian witness to address technological conditions that keep people poor and oppressed, recognizing the ways access to new technology and characteristics of the digital domain contribute to new forms of poverty and oppression.

54. Bostrom, "A History of Transhumanist Thought," 10.
55. Bostrom, "Human Genetic Enhancements," 503.

Jesus' good news did not merely speak to people's spiritual condition but "very much concerned the 'outer person' as well and the circumstances of human life: ordinary poverty, hunger, sickness, oppression, captivity, and so on (see Matt. 5:3–12; Luke 4:18–19; 6:20–26)."[56] In contrast to Bostrom's statement, Christian witness testifies that inequalities should not be justified, accepted, or ignored; rather they must be confessed and repented from, and steps need to continue to be taken to change unjust circumstances. Christian witness in a technological age must include social practices that testify to God's preference for the poor and the marginalized—the people most deeply impacted by inequalities and the injustice, oppression, and cruelty that parallel inequalities.[57] Preferential treatment of the poor—people who lack money, work, relationships, power, or status—is demonstrated in practices like generosity and mercy, and in sharing power and rejecting or transforming systems that privilege certain groups and dominate and persecute others.

In a technological age with desire for longer life-spans, Christian witness will need to include attention to the implications of longer life-spans for deepening disparities in three major categories of concern: wealth, consumption, and work.[58] Peters explains, "Money talks. What money says goes. No escape exists to liberate technological progress from the vested interests of the economic and political powers that make such progress possible. Despite their feeble whisperings of liberal values such as altruism, cooperation, and ecology, the progress transhumanists anticipate will be unavoidably diverted into the service of consolidating and expanding the wealth of its investors."[59] Alarms need to be sounded related to who will administer, regulate, and make money off of human enhancement and how each of these categories of concern might relate to power inequities, economic disparity, and injustice. Christians will need to testify to God's passion for justice for the "least of these" (Matthew 5:19, 25:40) by preaching for, prophesying about, and embodying distributive and restorative justice.

It is conceivable that having more and more people live forever will contribute to more profound consumption issues than we already have. Consumption issues are related to larger worries like climate change. It is

56. Volf and Croasmun, *Life of the World*, 72.

57. Cone, *God of the Oppressed*, 134–39.

58. Cole-Turner, "Transhumanism and Christianity," 194, in Cole-Turner, ed. *Transhumanism and Transcendence*.

59. Peters, "Progress and Provolution," 76.

possible that inhabited parts of Earth will become unlivable due to things like famine and natural disasters like hurricanes—likely consequences of overconsumption and climate change. If this happens, people will continue to be forced off their land. It is also plausible that there will be some parts of the Earth that are most conducive to human longevity and some people will be able to afford them and many people will not. In view of these possibilities, it is crucial that Christian witness include attention to negative outcomes of prolonged life that could contribute to more refugees and worse economic disparities.

Christian witness in a technological age should also be concerned with the nature of work and vocation in an age of enhanced humanity. Historian Yuval Noah Harari has written about the possibility of a "useless" class of people due to having no work (which is often related to vocation) as a result of biological inequality, people whose cognitive and physical abilities render them unemployable.[60] Christian witness needs to involve imaginatively responding to the new issues related to work and vocation that technology will create.

Technology Design

Addressing deepening disparities and issues like wealth, consumption, and work, ultimately means Christian communities need to discern ways to address technological design, though this is extremely difficult work. Christian communities need to be able to engage in public theology and articulate in compelling ways Christian visions of flourishing in a new media landscape. It is important to clearly articulate values, desires, and practices worth pursuing.[61] Christian communities can share publicly both in person and in mediated forms (videos, blogs, websites, social media) what sort of technology is worth making and encourage the creation of technology that nurtures a meaningful, loving life.

Members of Christian communities can also participate in advocacy work that hold technology companies accountable to designing new media that nurtures flourishing. Advocacy work can involve encouraging user-experience designers at tech companies to focus on creating design features of technology that invite activities that nurture connection rather

60. Harari, "Are we about to witness the most unequal societies in history?" See also Harari, *Homo Deus*.

61. Volf, "Conversation with Miroslav Volf," 0:21.

than contribute to diminished humanness and mental distress.[62] Christian communities can also choose to support and give money to tech companies or advocacy groups that are committed to advancing new technology that nurtures love. While most Christian communities are limited in their capacity to nurture changes in new media design, they can nonetheless advocate for and support these changes to the extent that they are able.

Interested Conversation

Addressing the issues that transhumanism raises related to meaningful ends, the body, suffering, inequality, and technology design requires Christian communities that are committed to an ongoing *interested conversation* about the dynamics of our technological landscape and how these dynamics are shaping people's identity formation, work, volunteerism, education, faith, politics, feelings, and relationships.[63] This means "*interest* in the Spirit's leading in this new technological landscape—not negativity, not unreflective enthusiasm, not assumptions. It is conversation that is genuinely interested in what God is doing in this landscape and interested in how new technology is impacting people's lives."[64]

Christians "behold and tell" about the life worth living within a community of pilgrims—people following and practicing a *way of life* seeking understanding—who try together to discern the Spirit leading.[65] Stroope explains, "Rather than adopting business or military techniques and strategies, and rather than outsourcing witness to experts or professionals, assemblies of pilgrims look to the Spirit's direction and power."[66] This assembly of pilgrims is actual in that it involves people who meet together regularly in physical and digital spaces, but this community is also connected to other Christian communities—local and around the world—as well as the cloud of witnesses throughout time that make up the historic Christian tradition.

Rather than relying solely on human reason and science, Christian communities realize they also need to respond to the Spirit's leading. Seeking to listen to and respond to the Spirit is perhaps one of the strangest

62. Gorrell, *always on*, 95.

63. Gorrell, *always on*, 33–35.

64. Gorrell, *always on*, 34–35.

65. Stroope, *Transcending Mission*, 371.

66. Stroope, *Transcending Mission*, 381.

qualities of Christian witness—it demands radical faith. However, it calls for no less faith than the faith it takes to believe human beings can control the future and reason their way to right action, for "faith of some kind is crucial to all human knowing and selfhood."[67]

Practical theologian Mark Lau Branson explains, "Whatever the nature or cause or impact of a disruption, God is always on the ground, among us, among our neighbors, initiating with love, hope, and (sometimes) judgment."[68] Christians witness to the belief that God is always among us, always initiating, always inviting and therefore, we must always parallel the question, "what should we do" with the question, "what is God doing?" Christians witness to the need to help one another to discern answers to questions like, "Which technological advancements are worth pursuing and what human improvements are worth wanting?" "How long should we live?"

Christian witness is shaped by a reliance on the Spirit of God to help communities to make sense of their experiences, and to critically and theologically reflect on tradition and Scripture, especially Jesus' life and teachings, in order to discern what we should do. In order to listen to God's voice, Christian communities engage in powerful social practices alongside of others, such as study, prayer, silence, fasting, storytelling, and testimony. No one is alone on the quest to discern God's leading and every person in the community matters. Communal discernment requires humility, an openness to being corrected, and the acceptance that sometimes we will inevitably get it wrong.

Eventually, interested conversation will need to explicitly involve communal discernment regarding technological transformations. Humanity+ promises "increased opportunity for individuals to shape themselves and their lives according to their informed wishes."[69] However, Stahl rightly points out that "Far too often, technologies that were created to be freely chosen become legally, or at least socially obligatory."[70] It is imaginable that a significant consequence of individuals having to decide how long to prolong their life could be even more emotionally and mentally taxing for people than it is today. It is already difficult for individuals and families to determine how much medical intervention human beings should allow

67. Stassen et al., *Authentic Transformation*, 192.

68. Branson, "Disruptions Meet Practical Theology."

69. Humanity+, "Transhumanist FAQ."

70. Stahl, "Tillich and Transhumanism," 190.

for. Life-affirming Christian witness involves invitations into communal discernment seeking the Spirit's guidance about technology design, development, use, transformation, and when necessary, rejection.

Christian Witness

It is essential in the coming years that Christian witness remains focused on telling and beholding about Jesus' invitation to life—the abundant life, the life worth living, the life that truly is life. A Christian vision of the good life emphasizes becoming fully human through attending to the life and teachings of Jesus and the leading of the Spirit and witnesses to the significance of participating in and therefore embodying God's unconditional love. The life worth living is a life that by God's grace practices God's love. Therefore, Christian communities witness to the significance of God's *love*, to human formation as *communal* and involving *self-transcendence*, and accordingly, the importance not just of the psychological, intellectual, and physical dimensions of people's lives, but also of the *relational* and *spiritual* aspects of humanity.[71]

Christian communities witness to God's love and grace with their commitments to the affirmation of the integrated person and dignity of all bodies as well as the celebration of diversity. Love demonstrates self-transcendence, which is also manifested in concrete social practices like forgiveness, compassion, and mercy. Christian witnesses also testify to the sources of suffering and holistic healing and the need for relief of the poor and justice for the oppressed. Finally, Christians recognize and embrace the need for community, prayer, and communal discernment in the quest to determine technological design and which technological transformations we should embrace in the critical quest of becoming fully human.

Bibliography

ACLOR Life Extension Foundation. "What is Cryonics?" Last modified 2019. https://alcor.org/AboutCryonics/.

Angelica, Amara D., ed. *The Ray Kurzweil Reader.* https://www.kurzweilai.net/pdf/RayKurzweilReader.pdf.

Baldwin, James. *James Baldwin: Collected Essays.* New York: Library of America, 1998.

Bostrom, Nick. "A History of Transhumanist Thought." *Journal of Evolution and Technology* 14.1 (April 2005) 4–5. https://www.nickbostrom.com/papers/history.pdf.

71. Zimmermann, "Human Flourishing."

———. "Human Genetic Enhancements: A Transhumanist Perspective." *Journal of Value Inquiry* 37.4 (2003) 493–506.

Branson, Mark Lau. "Disruptions Meet Practical Theology." Fuller Studio. https://fulerstudio.fuller.edu/disruptions-meet-practical-theology/.

Christian Transhumanist Association. "The Christian Transhumanist Affirmation." Last modified 2019. https://www.christiantranshumanism.org.

Cole-Turner, Ronald, ed. *Transhumanism and Transcendence: Christian Hope in an Age of Technological Enhancement.* Washington, DC: Georgetown University Press, 2011.

Cone, James. *God of the Oppressed.* Maryknoll, NY: Orbis, 1997.

Glover, Jonathan. *What Sort of People Should There Be?* London: Penguin, 1984.

Gorrell, Angela. *always on: practicing faith in a new media landscape.* Grand Rapids: Baker Academic, 2019.

H+Pedia. "Transhumanist Bill of Rights." Last modified December 9, 2018. https://hpluspedia.org/wiki/Transhumanist_Bill_of_Rights#Version_1.0.

Harari, Yuval Noah. "Are we about to witness the most unequal societies in history?" *The Guardian,* May 24, 2017. https://www.theguardian.com/inequality/2017/may/24/are-we-about-to-witness-the-most-unequal-societies-in-history-yuval-noah-harari.

———. *Homo Deus: A Brief History of Tomorrow.* New York: HarperCollins, 2017.

Humanity+. "Humanity+—What We Do." Last modified 2018. https://humanityplus.org.

———. "Transhumanist Declaration." Last modified 2018. https://humanityplus.org/philosophy/transhumanist-declaration/.

———. "Transhumanist FAQ." Last modified 2018. https://humanityplus.org/philosophy/transhumanist-faq/.

Huxley, Julian. *New Bottles for New Wine.* London: Chatto & Windus, 1957.

Kurzweil, Ray. *The Singularity Is Near: When Humans Transcend Biology.* New York: Penguin, 2005.

Mill, John Stuart. *Utilitarianism.* 4th ed. London: Longmans Green and Co., 1871.

Miller, Emily McFarlan. "Should we live to be 500? Christians and secularists come together over transhumanism." *Religion News,* September 2, 2018. https://religionnews.com/2018/09/05/should-we-live-to-be-500-christians-and-secularists-come-together-over-transhumanism/.

More, Max. "The Overhuman in the Transhuman." *Journal of Evolution and Technology* 21.1 (January 2010) 1–4. https://jetpress.org/v21/more.htm.

Nietzsche, Friedrich. *The Gay Science.* Translated by Thomas Common. Mineola, NY: Dover, 2006.

O'Connell, Mark. "600 Miles in a Coffin-Shaped Bus, Campaigning Against Death Itself." *New York Times,* February 9, 2017. https://www.nytimes.com/2017/02/09/magazine/600-miles-in-a-coffin-shaped-bus-campaigning-against-death-itself.html.

Pearce, David. "The Abolitionist Project." https://www.hedweb.com/abolitionist-project/index.html.

———. "The Hedonistic Imperative." https://www.hedweb.com/.

Peters, Ted. "Progress and Provolution: Will Transhumanism Leave Sin Behind?" In *Transhumanism and Transcendence: Christian Hope in an Age of Technological Enhancement,* edited by Ronald Cole-Turner, 63–86. Washington, DC: Georgetown University Press, 2011.

Pryor, Adam, and Devan Stahl, eds. *The Body and Ultimate Concern: Reflections on an Embodied Theology of Paul Tillich.* Macon, GA: Mercer University Press, 2018.

Shenk, Wilbert R. *The Transfiguration of Mission: Biblical, Theological, and Historical Foundations.* Eugene, OR: Wipf and Stock, 1993.

Sinnott-Armstrong, Walter. "Consequentialism." *The Stanford Encyclopedia of Philosophy,* Summer 2019. https://plato.stanford.edu/entries/consequentialism/#ClaUti.

Sorgner, Stefan Lorenz. "Transhumanism." In *Encyclopedia of Time: Science, Philosophy, Theology, & Culture,* edited by James Birx, 1376–86. Thousand Oaks, CA: Sage, 2009.

Stahl, Devan. "Tillich and Transhumanism." In *The Body and Ultimate Concern: Reflections on an Embodied Theology of Paul Tillich,* edited by A. Pryor and D. Stahl, 185–212. Macon, GA: Mercer University Press, 2018.

Stassen, Glen, D. M. Yeager, and John Howard Yoder. *Authentic Transformation: A New Vision of Christ and Culture.* Nashville: Abingdon, 1996.

Stone, Bryan. *Evangelism after Pluralism: The Ethics of Christian Witness.* Grand Rapids: Baker Academic, 2018.

Stroope, Michael W. *Transcending Mission: The Eclipse of Modern Tradition.* Downers Grove, IL: IVP Academic, 2017.

Swinton, John. "Many Bodies, Many Worlds." *Christian Reflection: A Series in Faith and Ethics.* https://www.baylor.edu/content/services/document.php/188190.pdf.

Tanner, Kathryn. *Theories of Culture: A New Agenda for Theology.* Minneapolis: Fortress, 1997.

Volf, Miroslav. "Conversation with Miroslav Volf." YouTube video, 0:21. Posted by Yale Divinity School. January 11, 2016. https://www.youtube.com/watch?v=OKtsoAlCPGk.

———, and Matthew Croasmun. *For the Life of the World: Theology That Makes a Difference.* Grand Rapids: Brazos, 2019.

Zimmermann, Jens. "Human Flourishing in a Technological World: The First Year." Christian Flourishing in a Technological World. Last modified 2018. https://www.christianflourishing.com/blog/2018/10/28/human-flourishing-in-a-technological-world-the-first-year.

Afterword

KUTTER CALLAWAY

*I can only answer the question "What am I to do?" if I can answer
the prior question "Of what story or stories do I find myself a part?"*

—Alasdair MacIntyre[1]

The essays in this volume interrogate a number of the stories that late-
modern persons are telling themselves as the twenty-first century
moves into its third decade. They don't tell the whole story (because there
isn't such a thing). Rather, they serve as entry points into the complex network of overlapping, interconnected, and intersecting realities that have
come to define contemporary life. Thus, by offering a unique perspective
on this particular moment in time, each essay provides an occasion for us
as individuals and as a society to ask (and attempt to answer) the question
"what am I to do?"

Needless to say, determining what one ought to do is never easy,
but it's an even more monumental task when faced with the kinds of unprecedented technological advances that seem to pervade each and every
proceeding of the late-modern world and continue to unfold at alarm-
ingly rapid speeds. If science fiction narratives are a trustworthy index
of an era's collective imagination regarding the promises of technology
(e.g., *DEVS*, *Westworld*, and *Tales From the Loop*), then a brooding sense
of inevitability hovers over much of contemporary life, which, in some
cases, has given way to a kind of ethical and spiritual resignation, if not

1. MacIntyre, *After Virtue*, 216.

outright apathy. After all, there's very little point in attempting to discern what story we are in, much less what we ought to do, when the basic structures and logics of the technologically determined world we are hurtling towards have already been established. Our only obligation or, for that matter, our only choice is to accept the terms and conditions (which most do without even bothering to read the fine print).

In certain respects, the goal of *Techno-Sapiens* was to bring together a diverse collection of voices in order to counter just this kind of technological fatalism while also avoiding an equally unhelpful (and ultimately naïve) utopianism. As editors of the volume, we (Ryan and Kutter) are neither Luddites nor futurists, which means that, from our perspective, we need not be paralyzed by fear of what is to comes. But neither are we willing to make overly confident claims regarding exactly what the techno-future holds. For a number of reasons, those working on the leading edge of technological change are often assumed to have some kind of preternatural ability to see into the future. Sadly, we possess no such insight. It's hard enough describing the present with any kind of accuracy, so we'll leave the soothsaying to the professionals and focus instead on what is taking place right now.

The challenge, of course, is that a book's afterword is supposed to point toward the future in light of the chapters that have preceded it. In fact, if there ever were a place to speculate about society's technological prospects without discretion, this would be it. We have chosen to resist this urge, not because we lack the capacity or courage to imagine the ways in which technology might give rise to future possibilities, but rather because the future—at least the technological future—is fundamentally open. To focus on the present moment and to ask "what are we to do?" is therefore not to ignore the future or disregard it, but rather to create the necessary conditions in the here and now for the future we hope will come—a future that would not, indeed could not, come to pass otherwise.

Still, while we are certain of little, what we can say with some measure of confidence about our present reality is that the development and proliferation of modern technologies have fundamentally reshaped the whole of human life. And as each of the contributors to this volume have suggested in their own way, the need for a robust and constructive response to the transformative effects of technology is now more urgent than ever. This is especially true given how fast all things technological continue to change and, as a consequence, the depth and pace at which they upend life as we know it. As our friend and colleague Barry Taylor likes to say, it isn't simply that things are changing. That has always been the case. Rather, in the Networked society, it is that change itself has changed.

Starting with these facts on the ground, this book has considered how we as human beings might be and become neighbors in ways that leverage the potential of modern technology while also countering its destructive tendencies. In doing so, it explored three primary questions: 1) Who is my (digital) neighbor? And for that matter, who am I? 2) How does social media allow us to love our (digital) neighbor? and 3) What does it look like to be and become a (digital) neighbor? By focusing on the ways in which technology encourages and/or inhibits the human capacity to love our neighbor, the essays in this collection have raised new and important questions regarding the ongoing transformation of human life in this increasingly networked and technologically mediated world. Although by no means an exhaustive account, we bring this volume to a close by identifying three types of questions that will continue to require our full attention as we attempt to navigate an unknown (and in a very real sense, unknowable) future. These distinct but overlapping categories each contain questions that are principally concerned with the human, the other, and the Sabbath.

The Human

As the boundary that once separated humans from machines becomes more and more permeable and, in some cases, dissolves entirely, traditional definitions of human personhood are proving to be inadequate. This is not a future problem. It is a present crisis, and unlike so many of our present-day crises, it is one that does not have a technological solution. Philosophers, theologians, and missiologists alike thus need to marshal the very best of their intellectual resources in order to develop more sophisticated definitions of personhood that are able to account for the never-ending cycle of technological change that will inevitably challenge or undermine previous paradigms. In other words, as the rate of technological advances ratchets up in the days, years, and decades ahead, the age-old question of "what does it mean to be human?" will only become more and not less important. The answers will of course need to be refined, reshaped, and recast over time, but the question itself remains inescapable.

The suggestion that our definition of human personhood will need to change might be unsettling for some, but in truth, it represents an opportunity rather than an obstacle, especially for people of Christian faith who understand the incarnate Christ to be the paradigmatic human. As several of the essays in this volume point out, the transhumanist picture of the human as bits of data that can be uploaded and downloaded onto various technological substrates without remainder is fundamentally sub-Christian. It's a gnostic vision that disregards the basic materiality of human flesh as constitutive of human personhood. In contrast, given its incarnational commitments, the Christian tradition understands the human to be necessarily embodied. On this view, the human just is a material body comprised of organic (i.e., it's not synthetic) human (i.e., it's not a giraffe's body) flesh (i.e., it's in-*carn*-ate).

It may very well be that one day in the not too distant future we will be capable of uploading something called "human consciousness" to another substrate. And while that would certainly be an interesting development, it would produce something that is importantly not a human. To make this distinction is not to diminish these hybrid arrangements or to treat them as intrinsically inferior. It is rather to distinguish them from human beings in order to know how human persons might best relate themselves to these new forms of technological life.

All this to say, the challenge to human personhood that emerging technologies will continue to represent is less of an existential threat to Christianity than it is a strategically opportune moment to advocate for the deeply Christian notion that embodiment is central to our understanding of what it means to be human. From a missiological perspective, it also serves as a unique and perhaps even unparalleled opportunity to explore a variety of new and unexpected partnerships. For instance, Christians will find both secular humanists and persons from other religious traditions to be critical allies who share a common concern, namely, resisting the disembodied impulses of certain technological innovations. In this way, driven in part by advances in technology, groups traditionally thought to be diametrically opposed might find themselves forging ad hoc alliances based upon their collective commitment to the embodied nature of human persons.

The Other

If the question of what it means to be human skews a bit philosophical, the question of how we ought to love our digital neighbor is eminently practical, for it has to do with the ethics of navigating a landscape populated by both human and nonhuman others. It is therefore significant that, as it concerns nonhuman others in particular, many otherwise fruitful conversations have become overly focused on the anthropomorphized visions of artificial intelligence that are the hallmark of science fiction, raising the question of what it means for humans to regard these artificial others with compassion, empathy, and dignity. Again, who knows what the future may hold, but in terms of the present realities that threaten our ability to treat others empathetically (whether artificial or not), a far more probable and pressing matter concerns the faceless algorithms that aggregate our data, manipulate our behavior online, and profit from the very divisive and dehumanizing practices they incentivize.

This is no small matter, and it only underscores the importance of making critical distinctions between and among the variety of tools, media, systems, and social practices that are often lumped into a single category called "technology." There are important differences, for example, between the technological *devices* we use (e.g., the iPhone), the multinational *corporations* profiting from our online activities (e.g., Apple, Google, Amazon), the various *platforms* organizing our social networks (e.g., Facebook, Instagram, Twitter, etc.), and the basic *architecture*—the superstructure—of the increasingly participatory, user-generated digital world we inhabit on a day-to-day basis. These differences matter, not only for people of faith attempting to be wise and discerning consumers, users, and developers of technology, but also for a broader society moving into uncharted waters.

For instance, as Jaron Lanier has pointed out, numerous digital technologies can and indeed do function in constructive and life-giving ways (he's particularly fond of podcasts). However, the world we see when we log in to our social media platform of choice is one that prevents us from truly seeing the human other because it has been completely customized by algorithms (i.e., nonhuman others) that privilege "impressions" over everything else.[2] Unsurprisingly, the content that either aligns with our hyper-individualized preferences or is radically opposed to our preconceptions tends to generate the most "impressions." Making matters worse, advertising dollars artificially amplify this polarization, which means that Facebook, Instagram, Twitter, SnapChat, et al. have sold our eyeballs millions of times over to corporations more than willing to show us nothing other than posts that either reinforce everything we already believe or represent the polar opposite. In the end, what emerges is our own fully customized (and

---

2. Lanier, *Ten Arguments for Deleting Your Social Media Accounts Right Now.*

hyper-partisan) view of the world to which no other individual has access. Neither can we see what anyone else's feed looks like.

It might be tempting to say that these systems and their underlying structures are simply broken and that the Christian calling is to work at fixing what's broken so that we might be able to love our digital neighbors in and through these technologically mediated contexts. The only problem with this kind of vision is that the system isn't actually "broken" at all. It's working perfectly. It's doing exactly what it was designed to do. The current architecture is designed not only to incentivize but also to profit from our dehumanization of the other. All the while, it aims to convince us that there's no use pursuing liberation from its underlying logic because there is nothing to be freed from. This is simply "the way things are." Thus, if the cultivation of empathy begins and ends with our ability to see the world through the eyes of the other—even if just for a moment—then people of Christian faith will need to radically rethink their participation with digital networking platforms that make this empathetic gesture toward the other literally impossible, and imagine instead new forms of technological life that generate rather than inhibit human flourishing.

The Sabbath

Recall that you were slaves in the land of Egypt and that the LORD your God brought you out of there by strength and power. That is why the LORD your God has commanded you to observe the Sabbath day.

—Deuteronomy 5:15 (NET)

Recall for a moment the discussion in chapter 5 regarding the relationship between character formation and sabbath rest. It was rightly observed that, in the account found in the book of Exodus, the rationale for observing the Sabbath is that God rested on the seventh day of creation (Exodus 20:11). In Deuteronomy, however, Sabbath keeping is connected to the Exodus from Egypt. Sabbath rest, it would seem, is about more than recovering the energy we expend during the workweek. It has something to do with resisting the oppressive systems and structures within which we operate. Sometimes our participation in these power structures is willful, but more often than not, we are completely unaware of just how complicit we have become.

For this very reason, during a recent Lenten season, I (Kutter) chose to fast not from technology, but from social media in particular. I needed to observe the Sabbath. I needed to rest. I needed to resist. Of course, as one of our colleagues at Fuller Seminary says, "Fasting from social media is part of the modern world survival toolkit. Right next to using the do not disturb feature on your phone and YouTube tutorials."[3] But that's exactly the point of Sabbath keeping, isn't it? It's a routine (and somewhat mundane) reminder to ourselves and to others that we are not to be held captive by life-denying structures of power, no matter what form they might take. It's to remember that it is God and not Pharaoh whom we serve. In my particular case, to observe the Sabbath was to actively resist the influence of digital platforms that demonstrate very little concern for our bodies or our basic ability to empathize with others.

The theological twist, however, is that, just as Karl Barth would say, there is always a yes embedded in our no.[4] And as it concerns the technological future that is already here but yet to come, our yes involves what is potentially a radical embrace of technologies that provide us with the means for pursuing "what makes for peace and for building up one another" (Romans 14:19). From this perspective we need not be overly cautious or unduly concerned about technology. In fact, we can confidently affirm the transformative potential of certain technological innovations, especially those that lead to human flourishing. That being said, no technology is merely a neutral tool. Each has a purpose, a design—a telos—that makes it more or less suitable for liberating people from the unjust rhythms that define much of contemporary life. The question moving forward then, is not so much how we might periodically unplug ourselves from technology in order to "rest," but how we might actively pursue the welfare—the shalom—of the marginalized, the alien, and the other by practicing a technologically mediated form of Sabbath resistance. For, in the final analysis, it will be in the process of asking and answering that question that we will discover not only who our (digital) neighbor is and how to love them, but also what it means to be and become techno-sapiens ourselves.

3. Thanks to Aaron Dorsey for his wisdom.
4. Barth, *The Epistle to the Romans*.

Bibliography

Barth, Karl. *The Epistle to the Romans.* 6th ed. Translated by Edwyn C. Hoskyns. New York: Oxford University Press, 1968.

Lanier, Jaron. *Ten Arguments for Deleting Your Social Media Accounts Right Now.* New York: Henry Hold and Company, 2018.

MacIntyre, Alasdair. *After Virtue.* 3rd ed. Notre Dame, IN: University of Notre Dame Press, 2007.

Made in the USA
Las Vegas, NV
04 May 2023

71528698R00094